The
WIGGLESWORTH
Standard

The WIGGLESWORTH *Standard*

Peter J. Madden

 Whitaker House

Whitaker House thanks the Home of Peace, Oakland, California, for providing portions of the Smith Wigglesworth material included in this book.

THE WIGGLESWORTH STANDARD

ISBN: 0-88368-612-0
Printed in the United States of America
© 1993 by Whitaker House

Whitaker House
30 Hunt Valley Circle
New Kensington, PA 15068
Visit our web site at: www.whitakerhouse.com

Library of Congress Cataloging-in-Publication Data

Madden, Peter J., 1961–
   The Wigglesworth standard / written and compiled by Peter J. Madden
     p. cm.
   Includes bibliographical references (p.).
   ISBN 0-88368-612-0 (tradepaper : alk. paper)
    1. Wigglesworth, Smith, 1859–1947. 2. Christian Life—Pentecostal authors. I. Title.
   BX8762.Z8 W54 2000
   289.9'4'092—dc21
   [B]   00-036653

3 4 5 6 7 8 9 10 11 12 13 14 / 10 09 08 07 06 05 04 03 02

DEDICATION

☙

To Lia,
my loving wife
and greatest support

ACKNOWLEDGMENTS

The author gratefully acknowledges the Home of Peace, Oakland, California, for providing the Smith Wigglesworth sermons included in this book, which were originally published in *Triumphs of Faith*.

In addition, the author wishes to express his heartfelt gratitude to Gospel Publishing House in Springfield, Missouri, for their generous permission to use information found in the following books: *Smith Wigglesworth: Apostle of Faith* by Stanley Frodsham, *Seven Pentecostal Pioneers* by Colin Whittaker, and *Ever Increasing Faith* and *Faith That Prevails* by Smith Wigglesworth.

Credit needs also to be expressed to Harrison House in Tulsa, Oklahoma, for granting permission to quote from these publications: *Smith Wigglesworth Remembered* by William Hacking, *Smith Wigglesworth: The Secret of His Power* by Albert Hibbert, and *Smith Wigglesworth: A Man Who Walked with God* by George Stormont.

Finally, thanks are extended to Servant Publications in Ann Arbor, Michigan, for allowing the use of historical details from Jack Hywel-Davies' book, *The Life of Smith Wigglesworth*.

Contents

INTRODUCTION

*Clearly you are an **epistle of Christ**,...
written not with ink but by the Spirit of the
living God, not on tablets of stone but on tablets
of flesh, that is, of the heart.*
—2 Corinthians 3:3, emphasis added

Smith Wigglesworth constantly preached this truth, which was definitely exhibited by his own life. He was truly a living *"epistle of Christ."* As we look at the heart and message of this great man of faith, we learn some wonderful lessons and read some great and mighty things on the pages of his life.

The very first time I heard of Smith Wigglesworth, the Holy Spirit stirred within me and said, "I have a special message for you written on the life and testimony of this man that will affect your whole life and ministry. Go and learn about him!"

This happened in my first few weeks of Bible college in Sydney, Australia. Two of my fellow students were discussing Wigglesworth during our lunch break. I was drawn to their conversation like iron to a magnet. That afternoon I bought my first book on this great man of faith. It was Stanley Frodsham's *Apostle of Faith*. I read it in a few days and then re-read it. In the months that followed, I bought every book I could find about him, and God spoke to me in a wonderful way through his life.

In those days, I would literally run home from the bus after a day at Bible college, lock myself in my room, turn off the lights, pull down the blinds, and seek the face of God for hours. My whole life became consumed with an intense hunger for God, and I lived for the times that I could be alone to pray. As the Word became increasingly more powerful and real to me, I began to walk in a new level of spiritual authority, as the Holy Spirit's anointing on my life intensified.

I began to talk to others about Wigglesworth, his relationship with God, and the miracles of healing that God worked through him wherever he went. Wigglesworth became such a topic of conversation with me that the other students would greet me with comments like "Here comes Wigglesworth." God used this man very much in my life and in the forming of the ministry He was to give me. I believe He wants to do the same in many others also.

There have been many other great living "epistles of Christ," men and women like Wesley, Finney, Booth, Hyde, Moody, Woodworth-Etter, Bosworth, Studd, Lake, Müller, Murray, Semple MacPherson, Simpson, Goforth, Kuhlman, and many others. They are all great living letters written by the hand of God, letters we do well to read and follow, letters that I have studied and read, learned from and loved. In fact, the Word of God instructs us to honor them and follow their examples. They all have tremendous things to add to our lives. The Smith Wigglesworth epistle has some very special lessons and applications for us, things that I believe are very much needed in the body of Christ today.

Early in 1989, while I was serving as a pastor in the city of Wollongong, in Australia, the Holy Spirit prompted me to compile quotes from Wigglesworth's preaching. I thought that this was for my own inspiration and reference for preaching. But, as I began to compile the material, I felt the Lord wanted me to share it with others.

Not satisfied with just the existing published information on Wigglesworth, I began to look for fresh material. I checked sources in Australia and wrote to England, but without success. Discouraged, I put the project on a back burner and concentrated on other things.

Six months later, my family and I traveled to America on a completely different project. We stayed at the Home of Peace, an old missionary home in Oakland, California, where many great men and women of God have stayed in years past. To my great delight, I discovered that Wigglesworth had stopped there on numerous occasions. In fact, the founders of the Home of Peace, Mr. and Mrs. Montgomery, were close personal friends of his.

I began to sense that the Lord was doing something, and I soon found out what it was. God had brought me halfway around the world, some 13,000 miles from Australia to California, to an old house where, in a little old cupboard in the front room, I found what I had been looking and praying for: thirty-seven messages from God's apostle of faith, Smith Wigglesworth.

This book is written around these sermons. The lessons that the Holy Spirit taught me through the life and revelation given to Smith Wigglesworth, starting those many years ago at Bible college, are lessons that I believe He wants to bring to many believers today. This book is for those who want more of God, who want to be part of God's "end-times army" and who are prepared to become "flames of fire." (See Hebrews 1:7.) My prayer is that some of the fire, some of the hunger and revelation, some of the anointing and power on this man's life may become yours, and that God may be truly glorified.

> This book is for those who want more of God,…who are prepared to become "flames of fire."

MY ENDEAVOR

Smith Wigglesworth was a man with a striking and awesome revelation of Jesus Christ, a man who walked close to God. Only an intimacy beyond the normal, an intimacy deep and rich and real, a closeness, almost a oneness with the Holy Spirit, could produce such a powerful insight into divinity, bring such miraculous power to heal the sick and raise the dead, develop such an incredible faith—a faith that would change the Christian world—and bring a man to such brokenness and to such a deep consciousness of his own nothingness before God.

My endeavor is not to glorify this man, for God shares His glory with no man. His own glory was the last thing that Smith Wigglesworth wanted, for he only desired to give glory to God.

However, in Christ, and under the direction of the Holy Spirit, my undertaking in writing this book is to challenge your commitment to Jesus Christ, to build and inspire your faith, to ignite your zeal, to deepen your compassion, to enlarge your heart and mind, and to explode your vision through a study of this man, his life, his theology, and his principles of faith. An evangelist, an apostle of faith, forefather of the Pentecostal church, Smith Wigglesworth was a living epistle of God in the twentieth century.

Chapter One

FLAMES OF FIRE

PROLOGUE
⚛
"That You May Marvel"

"While staying in the home of a curate of the local Church of England, [Wigglesworth] and the curate were sitting together talking after supper. No doubt the subject of their conversation was that the poor fellow had no legs. Artificial limbs in those days were unlike the sophisticated limbs of today.

"Wigglesworth said to the man quite suddenly (which he often did when ministering in cases like this), 'Go and get a pair of new shoes in the morning.'

"The poor fellow thought it was some kind of joke. However, after Wigglesworth and the curate had retired to their respective rooms for the night, God said to the curate, 'Do as My servant hath said.' What a designation for any person—*My servant!* God was identifying Himself with Wigglesworth.

"There was no more sleep for the man that night. He rose up early, went downtown, and stood waiting for the shoe shop to open. The manager eventually arrived and opened the shop for business. The curate went in and sat down.

"Presently an assistant came and said, 'Good morning, sir. Can I help you?'

"The man said, 'Yes, would you get me a pair of shoes, please.'

"'Yes, sir. Size and color?'

"The curate hesitated. The assistant then saw his condition and said, 'Sorry, sir. We can't help you.'

"'It's all right, young man. But I do want a pair of shoes. Size 8, color black.'

"The assistant went to get the requested shoes. A few minutes later he returned and handed them to the man. The man put one stump into a shoe, and instantly a foot and leg formed! Then the same thing happened with the other leg!

"He walked out of that shop, not only with a new pair of shoes, but also with a new pair of legs!

"Wigglesworth was not surprised. He had expected the result. He often made remarks like this: 'As far as God is concerned, there is no difference between forming a limb and healing a broken bone.'"[1]

FLAMES OF FIRE

What was this awesome power that moved through evangelist Smith Wigglesworth? Of course, it was the power of God. Why was it so prolific in his life? The only way we can understand this is to study the Wigglesworth epistle. To do so, we need to look at both the life he lived and the message he preached.

Paul said, *"Imitate me, just as I also imitate Christ"* (1 Corinthians 11:1). He didn't just say, "Do what I say," but he said, "Do what I do." In the same way, it is important for us to look at what Wigglesworth did, as well as what he said; therefore, we will begin by examining his life.

THE LIFE STANDARD:
Wigglesworth's Early Years

Smith Wigglesworth was a *"flame of fire"* (Hebrews 1:7), a man burning with the Spirit of God. He burned with a passion to know God and to commune with Him. He burned with a passion for God's Word, for souls, for Holy Spirit manifestation, for holiness, and for Christlikeness.

Born in 1859 in a humble shack in the small village of Menston, in Yorkshire, England, Wigglesworth was one of four children. Because the family was poor, he started work at the age of six to help support the family. His childhood was filled with long hours of hard work, yet he grew up in an atmosphere of simplicity and happiness.

At the age of eight, the young Wigglesworth received a clear knowledge that he was born again through the blood of Jesus Christ. As he stood clapping around a wood stove in an old-time Wesleyan Methodist church with his grandmother and others, he made Jesus Christ the Lord of his young life.

As he grew physically, his hunger and passion for God increased correspondingly. This hunger was the primary foundation for the power that was later to be manifested so radically in his life and ministry.

As you will see in the messages in this book, he desired to instill in others the same hunger that burned so strongly in him, for he understood its great importance. To hunger after God, to never be satisfied with his present position, to press on to the fullness of the Spirit—these were the foundations of Wigglesworth's life.

At his conversion, his hunger for the salvation of souls began. The first person that he won to Christ was his own mother. From there he continually tried to bring Christ to all the boys that he knew. He received many rebukes and rebuffs in his early years, but he never lost his burning desire to draw people to his Savior.

At the age of thirteen, he moved with his family to Bradford, England, where he again attended a Wesleyan Methodist church. His keenness for God must have been evident, for he was one of seven boys chosen to speak at the special missionary meetings that were being held at his church. Although he was only asked to talk for fifteen minutes, he lived in earnest prayer for weeks before the event. When the time came for him to speak, he was burning with a mighty zeal and a great desire for souls to be saved.

When Wigglesworth was sixteen, the Salvation Army came to Bradford. The Army, under the leadership of General William Booth, was a fresh and powerful evangelistic movement that delighted young Wigglesworth, for he found in its people a kindred spirit to his own in their earnestness to lead people to Christ and their great desire for God.

At this young age, he began a season of prayer and fasting for souls as the Holy Spirit led him further. Every week he joined his faith with that of the Salvation Army brothers and sisters, and they saw dozens yield their lives to Christ.

Wigglesworth realized from a young age that salvation is the heartbeat of God. Faith for souls must become priority, first priority, and it was out of this priority that his journey of faith began.

Wigglesworth stayed with the Army for several years. He saw that they had God's power, which he fervently desired. During their fiery prayer meetings, many people would fall down under the power of the Holy Spirit for long periods, sometimes twenty-four hours. They also saw results from their prayers. Because they believed God for a specific number of people to be saved each week, God rewarded their faith with that number!

Wigglesworth wanted to be in the center of what God was doing, so he went with those who were moving in the greatest blessing at the time, following loyalty to God rather than loyalty to man or any particular institution. He had the needed flexibility to move with God rather than chasing vanity. Because he knew that *"by their fruits you will know them"* (Matthew 7:20), he went where he saw the fruit.

We can see in Wigglesworth's life that the establishment of the kingdom of God and the salvation of souls were his primary concerns from an early age. These passions continued throughout his life, except for a brief period when his business made a "takeover bid" for top-priority position.

Many Christians start in the same way, zealous for God and for souls, full of love and compassion, hungry for the Word and for power, declaring that God will always be "number one" in their lives. This is the way it should be. The sad thing is that not many continue in this way, in what Jesus called *"your first love"* (Revelation 2:4).

Live in *"first love"* for Christ.

Jesus said that he had *"this against"* the church at Ephesus because they had *"left* [their] *first love"* (v. 4). But we don't have to live in Ephesus; *"first love"* doesn't have to die, and the "honeymoon" period doesn't have to come to an end. In fact, we are to progress continually in love, in zeal, in passion, in burning desire, in joy, and in excitement about Jesus. "[His mercies] *are new every morning"* (Lamentations 3:23), and our love for Him and revelations of Him should be also.

Wigglesworth lived in newness of life, in *"first love."* The message we read in his life is a continuing love, a continually increasing desire for God and His kingdom. This is the first key to the walk of power!

You may say, "Well, Wigglesworth was a special case. I can't be like him." But the reality is that it is your decision. Jesus said to the church at Ephesus in Revelation 2:5 that they were to *"repent and do the first works,"* showing clearly that living in *"first love"* is a decision that we have to make, and not something that God puts on a special few.

God is raising up a generation of people in these last days who have made the decision to be "flames of fire," burning with *"first love"* and holy desire, and they will change the face of this world for Jesus!

As you study the following powerful message given by Smith Wigglesworth, see the man behind it. He called himself "the thirstiest man in the world." Open your heart to the hunger he had, and pray that it will be imparted to your life, that you will begin a new phase toward the walk of power.

****

Flames of Fire
A Message by Smith Wigglesworth

Praise the Lord! I am sure anyone would have great liberty in preaching in this convention! I believe God the Holy Spirit can so bring into our hearts these truths that we shall live in the top place of expectation.

There may be much variation in these meetings, but I believe God will give us the desire of our hearts.

I am so glad to be here — my heart is full on so many lines. The message to me this morning was very fine.

I know that only God can satisfy my thirst. I know this: the man who is to be possessed with a zeal for God's work can only possess it as he is thirsty after God. Jesus had a great longing — a great passion. It was the zeal of the house of God.

I believe that this morning God wants to bring us to a place where we shall realize there is a revolution coming in our lives. Oh, beloved, it seems to me that we shall never be anywhere for God until there has been perfect revolution in our whole being.

It was a tremendous thought for me to know that I had received the Holy Spirit, but I am coming to a great wonderment of splendor to know that the Holy Spirit has at last got me! And the revolution has had such an effect upon my life that everything is of new order — a reviving process — a divine mark right within the inner heart. It is certainly an incision without a mark, but God puts His stamp into the hidden desires and cravings, and the whole thing is a great plan of a divine creation — the thirst of God after the image of the one He first created. It was forfeited, but it is now being brought back to its beginning. It may only be in its infancy, but, oh, the development since last year of God's incarnation in my whole soul.

Nothing less will please the Lord, only a constant, full burnt offering for God, where He is in absolute and utter authority over my whole being, until I am living, thinking, acting in the power of the Holy Spirit. Praise the Lord!

It is worthy of thought this morning, to allow God to bring a powerful might to so burst upon all our natural desires and longings so that we may at last come onto a plane of the divine plan where God breathes His own breath and makes His own food and eats and drinks with us and lives within us, an overflowing measure that shall never be taken away.

There is something in this Pentecostal work for God that it seems a continual decreasing with an increasing measure to take over the measureless measure! I am satisfied in my heart this morning that the hand of God is upon us. If we could only believe to see the glory of the salvation that God has got for us in the person of Jesus!

Shall we read the first chapter of Hebrews? It is full of holy vision. The word that I have for you this morning is in the seventh verse:

> *And of the angels He says: "Who makes his angels spirits and his ministers a flame of fire."*
> *(Hebrews 1:7)*

His ministers are to be *"flame[s] of fire"*! This means so much for us this morning. It seems to me that no man with a vision, especially a vision by the Spirit's power, can read that wonderful verse, that divine truth, without being kindled to such *"a flame of fire"* for his Lord that it seems as if it would burn up everything that would interfere with its progress.

"A flame of fire"! A perpetual fire, a constant fire, a constant burning, a holy inward flame that is exactly that which God's Son was in the world manifesting for

us all. I can see this: that God has nothing less for us than to be flames! The import of our message is that the Holy Spirit has come to make Jesus King.

It seems to me that the seed, which is an eternal seed, that life that was given to us when we believed, was of such a nature of the resurrection power that I see a new creation rising with a kingly position, and I see that when the Holy Spirit comes, He comes to crown Jesus King. So, beloved, it is not only the King within, but all the glories of the kingly manifestations that are brought forth.

So I see this: that even that alone would cause you to feel a burning after Jesus, a longing, a passion after Him. Oh, for Him to so work in us, melting us until a new order rises, moved with compassion!

There is something about the message that I want you to catch this morning. It does not seem to me that God can in any way even make us to be anything. But I do see that we can so come into a place in the order of God that He sets us up where the vision becomes so much brighter and where the Lord is in His glory with all His beatitudes and gifts, and all His glory seems to fill the soul who is absolutely dead to self and alive to Him.

There is so much talk about death, but I see that there is a death that is so deep in God, that out of that death God brings the splendor of His life and all His glory.

A remarkable evidence of being *"a flame of fire"* (Hebrews 1:7) for God came when I was traveling from Egypt to Italy. It is quite true when I tell you that on the ship and everywhere God has been with me. A man on the ship suddenly collapsed. His wife was in a terrible state, and everybody else seemed to be, also. Some said that it had come to an end, but, oh, to be a flame—to be indwelt by the living Christ! We are a back number if we have to pray for power, if we have to wait until we feel a sense of His presence. The baptism in the Holy Spirit should empower you for any emergency.

> *You shall receive power when the Holy Spirit has come upon you.* *(Acts 1:8)*

Within you there is greater power than there is in the world. Oh, to be awakened out of our place of unbelief into a place of daring for God! On the authority of the blessed Book!

So in the name of Jesus, I rebuked the demon, and to the astonishment of the man's wife and himself, he was able to stand.

He said, "What is this? It is going all over me. I have never felt anything like this before," for from the crown of his head to the soles of his feet, the power of God shook him.

"Be ready in season and out of season" (2 Timothy 4:2). God has for us an authority over the powers of the Devil—over all the powers of the Enemy. Oh, that we may live in the place where the glory excels!

I so desire that we could all see Him this morning. God says to us through His lovely Word,

*Who being the brightness of His glory and the ex-
press image of His person, and upholding all things
by the word of His power, when He had by Himself
purged our sins, sat down at the right hand of the
Majesty on high.* (Hebrews 1:3)

It would make anyone *"a flame of fire."* Praise God,
it is a fact! Jesus is in our bodies, and He is the express
image of God, and He has come to our human weakness to change us into a divine substance, so that by
the power of His might we may not only overcome,
but rejoice in the fact that we are more than overcomers. God wants us to have the last part—more
than overcomers!

Beloved, all that I speak this morning is burning
in my soul. The baptism of the Spirit has come for
nothing less than to eat the whole of my life. It set up
Jesus as King, and nothing can stand in His holy presence when He is made King. Everything will wither
before Him. I am realizing this.

I feel like I come to a convention like this to stir
you up and to help you to know that this inheritance
of the Spirit is given to every man to profit from.
Praise the Lord! And in the Holy Spirit order, we have
to come behind with no gifts, but I love the thought
that all the gifts are of no qualification or service to us
if the Giver does not work the gift.

If He is working the gift and it is there in operation, you are there only as an instrument or a voice or
a temple. He fills the temple; He fills the bill! Oh, it is
lovely! He dwells inside! He lives, He moves, He reveals. He causes us to forget our sorrow and *"rejoice
with joy unspeakable and full of glory"* (1 Peter 1:8 KJV).

"The brightness of His glory and the express image of His person" (Hebrews 1:3). We must not forget that we must make this a personal thing. When God made the angels, He made them sing. All that were in the heavens did obedience to this wonderful royal King, and, beloved, we must see that this Word this morning is a personal experience.

I look at the Scriptures, and I say, "Oh, Lord, it must be mine if You give it to me. You must make it mine." This is how I talk to Him, so He knows my language well! And I am the thirstiest man in the world, and He has a reservoir specially for me and for us all.

We sometimes get to a place where we say, "Lord, it is no good. Nothing you have shown me yet has moved me sufficiently. You will have to do something like You did in the Bible, something that will make the people marvel." *"Greater works than these, that you may marvel"* (John 5:20).

This same Jesus has come for one purpose, that He might be so manifested in us that the world shall see Him, and we must be burning and shining lights to reflect such a holy Jesus. We cannot do it with cold, indifferent experiences, and we never shall.

I come across people at times who always "have a good report," but, oh, for a Pentecostal ring in our hearts all the time! Oh, what you have got, brother, sister. It is His purpose to take you into the Promised Land.

What an inward burning, what an inward craving God can give! It is a taste of the heavenlies!

And we want more! More of the these heavenly joys, until God has absolutely put His stamp upon everyone by the power of His presence.

****

LIFE KEYS FROM THE SERMON

Praise God! What a mighty message from the heart of God. There is so much in these words for us today, if we will apply ourselves. We need to look closely at what Wigglesworth was saying in this sermon and see how it applies to us personally. To do this, let us look at some of the major points in the message. They are keys for God's "end-times army."

Key #1
EXPECTATION

I believe God the Holy Spirit can so bring into our hearts these truths that we shall live in the top place of expectation.

"The top place of expectation"! This is where Wigglesworth lived, and where God would have us all live.

Wigglesworth lived in the place of expectation. It is important to note that Wigglesworth started his message with expectation, for it is the ingredient that he knew people needed in order to fully receive the Word of God and, in so doing, receive faith to have their needs met.

We see so much more in a meeting when there is expectancy that God will move, and not just the presumption that it will be the same as before.

Expectation is the eager and confident anticipation that you will meet with God. It is the faith attitude that paves the way for God to move; it is the foundation that makes the church alive.

Wigglesworth here said that expectation comes from the truths of God being fixed in our hearts by the Holy Spirit. Expectation is not a feeling or emotion that can be pumped up by positive thinking, but a direct result of the coupling of the study of the Word of God with fellowship with the Holy Spirit.

We must learn to build expectancy in our hearts before we arrive at a service. If we will do this, not only will we receive greater blessings and miracles ourselves, but also our expectancy can increase the blessing on the whole meeting.

How do we build expectation in our lives? *"Faith comes by hearing, and hearing by the word of God"* (Romans 10:17).

Thank Him for each revelation. Meditate on it. Apply it specifically to you and your life. Commit yourself to do it and live by it.

Don't rush ahead in the pursuit of intellectual knowledge, but allow the Holy Spirit to build faith and expectation in you *"precept upon precept, line upon line"* (Isaiah 28:13).

As you read this book, read it expecting to grow, and allow the Holy Spirit to fix each truth in your heart according to this process. Then you will get the maximum out of it.

Key #2
THIRST FOR GOD

> I know this: the man who is to be possessed with
> a zeal for God's work can only possess it as he is
> thirsty after God.

As we have seen in Wigglesworth's early life, it was thirsting after God that was the foundation of his ministry. As he stated, this thirst is absolutely necessary for those who are to be really used of God. Those "possessed with a zeal for God's work" are the movers and shakers in the kingdom of God. They are the ones who accomplish great things doing His work.

As we hunger and thirst for God, we come into deepening levels of relationship with Him. Then He starts to unfold His plan for our lives and the work He has for us to do. The gifts or abilities that believers have do not ultimately qualify them to be men or women of God, but rather their desires toward God do so.

The enemy of our souls seeks to divert us at any cost from full effectiveness and anointing in doing God's work, for he knows the great damage a man or woman fully empowered by God can do to his kingdom, like the damage Wigglesworth did. Therefore, his continual effort and plan is to undermine or divert our hunger for God. He uses many devices, such as spirits of religiosity, apathy, pride, and fatigue— anything to weaken our hunger for God—so that he can limit our effectiveness for God.

Many gifted Christians are seemingly working for God, but their work all too often is not motivated by a hunger and thirst for God. Ministry is rendered powerless and ineffective if we allow it to be based on anything other than a deep spiritual hunger—not for ministry, but for God Himself.

"Ministry" can be based on many things:

➢ hunger for recognition
➢ hunger for acceptance socially within the church
➢ hunger for power and control over others
➢ hunger for money
➢ hunger to achieve righteousness by works

And the list goes on.

These are some of the traps that so many have fallen into, even after starting with a sincere hunger for God, because of the Enemy's continual onslaught against the key principle of hunger. We must learn to come before the Lord and check our motivations and what we are really hungering for in the things we do, *"lest Satan should take advantage of us; for we are not ignorant of his devices"* (2 Corinthians 2:11).

> **We need to maintain a deep longing for God.**

All of us need to maintain a deep longing for God. Some might even have to renew it totally. In both cases, the working out of this in our lives is the same. The fire of desire for God comes from communion with Him, and this always begins with discipline. We must set our wills, our minds, and our emotions every day to seek Him. As we continue to seek Him and His power, the longing for greater fellowship begins to grow. Desire and discipline work hand in hand: the discipline feeds the desire, and the desire feeds the discipline.

Wigglesworth, later in his life, would awaken at four o'clock in the morning to have communion and fellowship with his Lord. It was not so much that he dutifully made himself do it, but that the "burning desire" within tapped him on the shoulder every morning, and he got up to participate in his greatest delight.

Seek the Lord constantly in the Word. Seek Him faithfully in the prayer closet, praying in the Holy Spirit. Seek Him continually in praise and worship. Engage your heart to seek Him until you are "possessed with a zeal for God's work," burning with holy desire.

Key #3
POSSESSED BY THE SPIRIT

But I am coming to a great wonderment of splendor to know that the Holy Spirit has at last got me!

Wigglesworth pointed here to a very powerful truth, one that he preached with regular frequency. He could proclaim this truth because it was real in his own life. It is also one of the themes of this book.

To possess the Spirit of God is one thing, but it is quite another to be possessed by the Spirit of God.

Millions around the world have received the baptism in the Holy Spirit since the great outpouring at the beginning of the twentieth century. This is part of the preparation of the church, the bride, for the return of the King of Kings. Wigglesworth definitely preached this message of the last-days Pentecost throughout the world. He was one of the first in England to receive the infilling of the Holy Spirit during the early twentieth century—on October 28, 1907.

However, the beauty and power of his life came from the fact that he went on from there to the position that he is talking about here. A further place in the Spirit exists, a place of being controlled and possessed by Him. God really starts to use men and women when they become totally consumed by Him, to the extent that their thinking, their ways of acting, their praying, their worshiping, their all becomes Spirit-controlled. Their lives are no longer their own but His.

> Nothing less will please the Lord, only a constant, full burnt offering for God, where He is in absolute and utter authority over my whole being, until I am living, thinking, acting in the power of the Holy Spirit.

We know that many people are affected by evil spirits in our day. Now, many people are "demonized," or affected by them in certain restricted areas of their lives, yet they still carry on relatively normal activities, being bound just in those areas. For example, they may be "demonized" by a spirit of alcoholism, spirits of anger and rage, or spirits of lust, yet the evil spirits don't dominate or control their whole existences.

However, a very few people actually are possessed by a demon. Those possessed are in an asylum strapped to a table or in a straightjacket, because they have no personal control, because the demon spirit is controlling them.

In the same way, many Christians are "Holy Spiritized," still living according to their own plans most of the time, affected by God's Spirit in some aspects of their lives. But a few are actually possessed by the Holy Spirit. Those possessed are the ones who have given over total control to Him. *"The people who know their God shall be strong, and carry out great exploits"* (Daniel 11:32). These are the ones constantly in intercession, the ones controlled by God, who hear His every call and heed His every Word.

> God is looking for those who will come to the place of absolute surrender.

This is the second step of the baptism in the Holy Spirit that the church needs to take hold of. The last-days church, with the opposition that it is up against and the work it still has to do, must take hold of this further step of being Spirit-filled.

God is looking for those who will come to the place of absolute surrender. They will be the laborers used in the end-times harvest, the last great worldwide revival. They will be God's end-times army—not those with great ability or gifts who have the Holy Spirit, but *those who have God's ability because the Holy Spirit has them.*

If your desire is to be a member of this special "armed forces unit," it requires your absolute dedication. You need to be baptized in the Holy Spirit and receive the gift of tongues as a starting point. If you have not experienced this yet, seek the Lord for it. Then find someone who has, so that they might lay hands on you and pray for you. Do not stop until you receive it. Finally, consecrate yourself to the surrendered life to become part of God's end-times army and *"a flame of fire"* (Hebrews 1:7).

Key #4
"FLAMES OF FIRE"

His ministers are to be *"flame*[s] *of fire"*!...
"A flame of fire"! A perpetual fire, a constant fire, a constant burning, a holy inward flame that is exactly that which God's Son was in the world manifesting for us all.

In Exodus 3, Moses met with God on Mount Horeb. As he stood on *"holy ground"* (v. 5), he saw a great wonder—a bush that burned but was never consumed. This is how God showed Himself to Moses, and, in a similar way, this is how God shows Himself to the world, through and in us.

"A flame of fire" is an inward burning with love and compassion, zeal and fervor, prayer and praise, righteous anger against the Devil and all his works, and a holy desire to see the kingdom of God established and growing. On fire but never consumed, burning but never burned out, this inward flame is fueled by relationship with God and fellowship with the Holy Spirit. If the fire in our hearts is fueled by

Him, how can it burn out? If we are fueled by anything else, it will, though.

This "perpetual burning" is what burned inside Wigglesworth. It came, of course, out of his hunger and thirst, his inward craving for God, which he called "a taste of the heavenlies."

The great English revivalist, John Wesley, was once asked about his enormous success in open-air preaching in England, because huge crowds would gather to hear him. His much repeated response was, "Every morning I set myself alight and people come for miles to watch me burn!"

> *O God, You are my God; early will I seek You; my soul thirsts for You; my flesh longs for You in a dry and thirsty land where there is no water. So I have looked for You in the sanctuary, to see Your power and Your glory.*
> *(Psalm 63:1–2)*

Every morning, set yourself alight by seeking Him earnestly, so that you might be *"a flame of fire,"* and people will come for miles to watch you glow. "The yearning brings the burning."

Key #5
TO LIVE READY

> We are a back number if we have to pray for power, if we have to wait until we feel a sense of His presence. The baptism in the Holy Spirit should empower you for any emergency.

Wigglesworth lived ready at all times, for every situation and every emergency. He walked in the

Spirit, possessed by the Spirit of God and therefore always ready. We must learn to walk in such a manner.

We have seen that intense hunger is the basic foundation for this walk of power. The next step after hunger is discipline, for discipline is the fruit and the evidence of real hunger. Discipline causes us to build the house during the calm, to build our prayer lives in good times, and not just pray for power during crisis periods. Then we don't have to struggle to try to build it during the storms.

> Wigglesworth was always "burning," fueled by seeking God's presence.

Unfortunately, however, many people live from one crisis to the next, only turning to God with any real intensity during emergencies. Therefore they never develop the faith needed to walk consistently in victory. The faith that we need is the faith that is built *"precept upon precept, line upon line,...here a little, there a little"* (Isaiah 28:10).

Faith must be built up every day! Jesus Himself said that a man must *"take up his cross daily"* (Luke 9:23). Daily, not weekly. Not just on Sunday, but every day. This is the only way we can live ready. Remember, a weekly walk is a weak walk!

You must come to the place of daily building, with a daily denial of self, a daily discipline of reading and meditating on the Word of God, a daily habit of spending quality time in worship and waiting on Him, and a daily seeking of Him for more. You will find that any man or woman doing substantial things for God lives in these daily disciplines. A *"flame of fire"* is always burning, always ready.

Wigglesworth lived this daily walk. He was always burning, fueled by his continuous seeking God's presence. Thus, he lived empowered and ready to serve. You can have this walk of power if you will pay the daily price of discipline.

Many young men asked Wigglesworth how they could obtain great faith like he had. Wigglesworth simply answered from the Scripture, *"First the blade, then the ear, after that the full corn in the ear"* (Mark 4:28 KJV). Real empowering faith does not spring up overnight. Rather, it is built daily, seven days a week, 365 days a year.

Key #6
WHEN JESUS REIGNS

The baptism in the Holy Spirit has come for nothing less than to eat up the whole of my life. It set up Jesus as King, and nothing can stand in His holy presence when He is made King.

Here is the standard of the baptism in the Holy Spirit that Wigglesworth preached and lived by: "nothing less" than that which would "eat up the whole of my life." This is being possessed by the Holy Spirit.

Wigglesworth would frequently declare in his meetings, "Yes, filled with God. Yes, filled with God, / Emptied of self and filled with God."[2] Along with John the Baptist, he would say, *"He must increase, but I must decrease"* (John 3:30). He patterned his life on the following principle:

All of self, none of God.
Less of self, more of God.
None of self, all of God.[3]

The purpose of the Holy Spirit baptism is to make Jesus King of our lives. For Jesus really to be King, and not just a figurehead, the baptism must "eat up the whole of my life." Possession is when He is fully, totally, in control.

Wigglesworth was so dedicated to this reality that at times he refused to pray for the sick until he had partaken of communion. This was to ensure that Wigglesworth was dead, and that it was fully Christ in him who would minister. If this wasn't completely true, he knew that there would be no power. What a blessed reality.

Unfortunately, today's standard of the baptism in the Holy Spirit has dropped drastically from the standard that Wigglesworth preached and lived. A church will normally experience only what it receives through preaching and teaching:

➢ If faith is preached, faith will increase.
➢ If healing is preached, there will be healing in the church.
➢ If prosperity for God's children is preached, then the people will prosper.

The same principle holds for any of the truths and promises of God's Word, because *"faith comes by hearing, and hearing by the word of God"* (Romans

10:17). If people hear the Word of God pertaining to a particular promise or truth, their faith will be built for it, and they will receive according to their faith. However, if they do not hear the Word of God pertaining to that thing, their faith will not be built for it, so how can they receive?

Now, it is also true that if a lesser standard of any truth is preached, a lesser standard will be received. John Wesley instructed His young preachers, "Preach faith until you have it, and then because you have it, you will preach faith."[4] Wesley understood this concept: the standard preached will build faith in people, and even in the preacher, to strive for and reach that standard.

One of the purposes of this book is that Christians around the world might again sit under the preaching of this great man, Smith Wigglesworth. His standard of faith, dedication, power, holiness, and of the baptism in the Holy Spirit was of such a high level that both preachers and laymen need to rise to that standard—the standard that God established in his life.

When you begin to grasp this standard of the baptism in the Holy Spirit that Wigglesworth had, let it become yours also. Set it before your face, and let it become your vision. Don't stop until you have it. Hunger for it, and ask God for it. Let it eat up the whole of your life, that Jesus might be King!

> This same Jesus has come for one purpose: that He might be so manifested in us that the world shall see Him, and we must be burning and shining lights to reflect such a holy Jesus.

Chapter Two

"Lord, What Do You Want Me to Do?"

PROLOGUE
∞
An Urgent Telegram

During the early years of his ministry, Wigglesworth received a desperate telegram from a family in a town some two hundred miles away, pleading with him to come pray for a young woman. Without hesitation, Wigglesworth traveled the distance as quickly as possible.

Upon his arrival, Wigglesworth discovered that a young woman had become a raging demoniac. Her parents and husband were distraught with the situation. They could not even bring the baby to her to nurse, for fear of the harm she might do to herself or the infant.

The family led Wigglesworth up a staircase to a room where the young mother was on the floor, being held down by five men. Even though she was physically very frail, the evil power that controlled her was more than a match for all five.

As Wigglesworth entered the room, the evil spirits that possessed her stared out of her eyes and snarled at him, "We are many. You can't cast us out."

With complete calm, Wigglesworth firmly stated, "Jesus can. Greater is He that is in me than he that is in the world."

"She's ours. We won't give her up!" the demonic voices growled repeatedly, filling the house with hideous laughter.

Undaunted, Wigglesworth commanded, "Be quiet. In the name of Jesus, come out of her, you foul spirits!"

With a shriek and one last attempt to retain their grasp on the woman, thirty-seven different demonic spirits came out of her, giving their names as they exited. At the authority of the name of Jesus, the demons had to relinquish their territory, and the woman was totally delivered.

The fragile, exhausted wife was tenderly bathed and put to bed by a very grateful husband. She slept for fourteen hours while her family rejoiced at the power and love of a loving God.

The next morning, a beautiful young lady nursed her baby and then joined her parents, husband, and Wigglesworth in a celebration of what the Lord had done. As they ate together, they gave thanks that the Lord had spared no expense to send His servant on such an errand of mercy.[1]

"LORD, WHAT DO YOU WANT ME TO DO?"

Before reading this next sermon, it would again be a great advantage for us to look at the message as Wigglesworth worked it out in his own life. We can then see that he lived what he preached, and reinforce the message through the example of his life.

THE LIFE STANDARD:
Wigglesworth's Early Years (Cont.)

One of the great marks of Wigglesworth's early years was his desire to serve and be used of God in whatever way he could. *"What do You want me to do?"* (Acts 9:6) was his attitude from the moment of his conversion, the attitude of a willing servant.

> *But he who is greatest among you shall be your servant.*   *(Matthew 23:11)*

Wigglesworth was to become a great, fiery preacher, but as a youth he was not naturally talented in public speaking. When he preached at the Salvation Army meetings, his speech was always broken, and he would end up weeping before the people. He much preferred to serve in other ways than in the pulpit. He earnestly desired to be able to speak clearly and well, but he was not able. However, because he was broken and contrite in spirit, the Lord used him, gifted or not.

As a young man, Wigglesworth threw himself wholeheartedly into the work of the Salvation Army. He was mainly drawn by their evangelistic emphasis because this was the passion of his heart.

At one of the Army's evening meetings, in a dilapidated old theater in Bradford, Wigglesworth watched a beautiful young woman praying to God for her salvation. Polly Featherstone was the woman who would eventually teach him to read, encourage him in the ministry, and be the perfect partner for him in what God had planned.

From the time he heard her give her testimony, Wigglesworth knew that she was to be his. Polly was a vivacious and outgoing person. Rapidly, she became a great soulwinner and then a preacher, very much in demand for evangelistic meetings and Bible studies. She shared the same burden and passion that he had. In 1882, five years after he first saw her, they were married.

Smith and Polly were a ministry team now. Polly continually encouraged her husband to preach, which he repeatedly tried. Unfortunately, he found himself unable to express the longing in his heart. He would prepare for a week, praying and sweating over a message. However, when he actually stood up, read the opening Scripture, and began to say a few stammering words, he found he could not verbalize what was in his heart and would invite Polly or someone else to take over.

Even though he had limitations in his speaking abilities, he was tireless in his zeal for God. Wigglesworth often described the teamwork between Polly and himself in this way: her job was to draw the fish into the net with her preaching, and his was to land them at the altar, praying with them until they had the assurance of salvation.

Tirelessly, he served in whatever way he could around the Bradford Street Mission that he and Polly had established. After an outdoor evangelistic outreach session on Saturday afternoon, he attended a prayer meeting on Saturday night, then got up early Sunday morning to prepare the church for the Lord's Day services. He organized the winter heating, swept out the building, prayed over each seat as he dusted them, arranged the communion table, and then led the prayer before the morning service.

At the close of the Sunday evening gatherings, usually many came to the altar desiring personal ministry. After attending to all the spiritual needs, the Wigglesworths would arrive home rather late, but often the fellowship and hospitality in their home extended well into the night.[2]

Involved in the children's ministry at the Bradford Mission, Wigglesworth picked up little ones from the surrounding neighborhoods on a pony and brought them to church. In this attitude of a servant, the foundation was laid for the powerful worldwide ministry that was to come.

Wigglesworth's healing ministry began with this same desire to serve. For a time he had to go weekly to Leeds, a city near his own in northern England, to purchase supplies for his plumbing business. While there, he discovered a place where divine healing was being taught and the sick ministered to. Although somewhat skeptical and critical at first, he was full of compassion for the sick and needy.

As a successful businessman, he had the means to take these poor people from his own hometown to the city of Leeds for the healing ministry. So every Tuesday he collected several willing, desperate souls to transport them to the meeting. Observing his compassion and commitment to others, the leaders at this healing service attempted to convince him that he could minister healing in Bradford just as they were doing in Leeds. However, Wigglesworth didn't believe he could, so he kept bringing them to Leeds.

Finally, they left him in charge of a meeting while they went to the Keswick Convention. Wigglesworth thought he could just take charge of the meeting but have someone else speak. It didn't work. Everyone insisted that he was to lead the whole meeting, including delivering the sermon. Somewhat unwillingly, he did.

After he had finished, fifteen people came to the altar for ministry. Wigglesworth was perplexed. What else could he do but pray for them? So he stepped out and did just that. To his surprise, the first man he prayed for was healed! The man had hobbled in on a pair of crutches. Wigglesworth went on to pray for the others, and they too were instantly touched. Thus began a healing ministry that affected tens of thousands of lives around the world.

Wigglesworth's healing ministry didn't come out of any learned formulas or techniques, but out of a deep compassion for the sick and an earnest desire to do whatever he could do for God. The message we read here in Wigglesworth's life is that his ministry, like all true ministry, came from a desire to serve and to obey.

Jesus told us, *"He who is greatest among you shall be your servant"* (Matthew 23:11). A fresh revelation of this truth is sorely needed today in the body of Christ: men and women must get their eyes off position and recognition and yearn to serve—simply to be the best servants they can be. Then the emphasis on having to be seen and recognized would fade, while the nature of Christ, the ultimate Servant, would rise again in the church, so that we might meet the needs of a hurting and dying generation.

To effectively minister Christ to others, we need His nature, that of the ultimate Servant.

If truly you desire to be used of God to the maximum, please take hold of this truth. This is one of the most important lessons and keys to the walk of power—doing whatever we can with what we have, whenever and wherever the opportunity arises, doing so *"heartily, as to the Lord"* (Colossians 3:23).

In the natural man, Smith Wigglesworth did not start with an overabundance of talents and abilities, but as he fully gave what he had, God continued to increase it until he became a mighty evangelist. In the parable of the talents, the master said to the faithful servant who had used wisely what he had been given:

> *You have been faithful over a few things, I will make you ruler over many things.*
> *(Matthew 25:23)*

The principle that Jesus taught here is so clearly illustrated for us in this man's life. Oh, that we might learn this same servant attitude, so that God might likewise use us to build His kingdom.

Please first read Acts 19 to get the full benefit from the following message by Smith Wigglesworth.

****

Lord, What Do You Want Me to Do?
A Message by Smith Wigglesworth

As soon as Paul saw the light from heaven above the brightness of the sun, he said, *"Lord, what do You want me to do?"* (Acts 9:6). And as soon as he was willing to yield, he was in a condition where God could meet his need, where God could display His power, where God could have the man.

Oh, beloved, are you saying today, *"Lord, what do You want me to do?"*

The place of yieldedness is just where God wants us. People are saying, "I want the baptism. I want healing. I would like to know of a certainty that I am a child of God." And I see nothing, absolutely nothing in the way except unyieldedness to the plan of God.

The condition was met that Paul demanded, and instantly when he laid hands on them, they were filled with the Spirit and spoke in other tongues and prophesied. (See Acts 19:6.) The only thing needed was just to be in the condition where God could come in.

The main thing today that God wants is obedience. Where you begin yielding and yielding to God, He has a plan for your life, and you come into that wonderful place where all you have to do is to eat the fruits of Canaan. I am convinced that Paul must have been in divine order as well as those men, and Paul had a mission right away to the whole of Asia.

Brothers and sisters, it is the call of God. Oh, I believe God wants to stir somebody's heart today to obedience; it may be for China or India or Africa, but the thing God is looking for is obedience.

"Lord, what do You want me to do?"   (Acts 9:6)

Now God worked unusual miracles by the hands of Paul, so that even handkerchiefs or aprons were brought from his body to the sick, and the diseases left them and the evil spirits went out of them.
                                                    (Acts 19:11–12)

If God can have His way today, the ministry of somebody will begin; it always begins as soon as you yield. Paul had been bringing many people to prison, but God brought Paul to such a place of yieldedness and brokenness that he cried out, *"Lord, what do You want me to do?"*

Paul's choice was to be a bondservant for Jesus Christ. Beloved, are you willing that God shall have His way today? God said, *"I will show him how many things he must suffer for My name's sake"* (Acts 9:16). But Paul saw that these things were working out *"a far more exceeding and eternal weight of glory"* (2 Corinthians 4:17).

You people who have come for a touch from God—are you willing to follow Him? Will you obey Him?

When the Prodigal Son had returned, and the father had killed the fatted calf and made a feast for him, the elder brother was angry and said, *"You never gave me a young goat, that I might make merry with my friends"* (Luke 15:29). But the father said to him, *"All that I have is yours"* (v. 31). He could kill a fatted calf at any time. Beloved, all in the father's house is ours, but it will come only through obedience. And when He can trust us, we will not come behind in anything.

"God worked unusual miracles by the hands of Paul" (Acts 19:11). Let us notice the handkerchiefs that went forth from his body. That is, when he touched and sent them forth, God performed special miracles through them, and diseases departed from the sick, and evil spirits went out of them. Is it not lovely?

I believe that, after we lay hands on these handkerchiefs and pray over them, they should be handled very sacredly, even as people carry them. They will bring life, if they are carried in faith to a suffering one. The very effect of it, if you only believed, would change your own body as you carried it.

A woman came to me one day and said, "My husband is such a trial to me. The first salary he gets, he spends it in drink, and then he cannot do his work and comes home. I love him very much. What can be done?"

I said, "If I were you, I would take a handkerchief and would place it under his head when he went to sleep at night, and say nothing to him, but have a living faith."

We anointed a handkerchief in the name of Jesus, and she put it under his head. Oh, beloved, there is a way to reach these wayward ones.

The next morning on his way to work, he stopped for a glass of beer. He lifted it to his lips, but he thought there was something wrong with it, and he put it down and went out. He went to another saloon, and another, and did the same thing. He came home sober.

His wife was gladly surprised, and he told her the story, how the drink had affected him. That was the turning point in his life. It meant not only giving up drink, but it meant his salvation.

God wants to change our faith today; He wants us to see it is not obtained by struggling and working and pining.

The Father Himself loves you.   (*John 16:27*)

*He Himself took our infirmities and bore our sick-
nesses.* (Matthew 8:17)

*Come to Me, all you who labor and are heavy laden,
and I will give you rest.* (Matthew 11:28)

Who is the man who will take the place of Paul,
and yield and yield and yield, until God possesses
him in such a way that from his body virtue shall flow
to the sick and suffering?

It will have to be the virtue of Christ that flows.
Don't think there is some magic virtue in the handkerchief, or you will miss the virtue: it is the living faith
of the man who lays the handkerchief on his body,
and the power of God through that faith. Praise God,
we may lay hold of this living faith today: "The blood
has never lost its power."

As we get in touch with Jesus, wonderful things
will take place. And what else? We shall get nearer
and nearer to Him.

There is another side to it:

*Exorcists took it upon themselves to call the name of
the Lord Jesus over those who had evil spirits, saying, "We exorcise you by the Jesus whom Paul
preaches."...And the evil spirit answered and said,
"Jesus I know, and Paul I know; but who are you?"*
(Acts 19:13, 15)

I plead with you in the name of Jesus, especially
those of you who are baptized, to awaken to the fact
that you have power, if God is with you; but there
must be a resemblance between you and Jesus.

The evil spirits said, *"Jesus I know, and Paul I know; but who are you?"* Paul had the resemblance to Christ.

You are not going to get it without having His presence; His presence changes you. You are not going to be able to get the results without the marks of the Lord Jesus.

A man must have the divine power within himself. Devils will take no notice of any power if they do not see the Christ: *"Jesus I know, and Paul I know; but who are you?"* The difference between these men and Paul was they did not have the marks of Christ, so the manifestation of the power of Christ was not seen.

Do you want power? Don't take it the wrong way. Don't take it as power because you speak in tongues. If God has given you revelations along certain lines, don't take that for the power. Even if you have laid hands on the sick and they have been healed, don't take that for the power. *"The Spirit of the LORD is upon Me"* (Luke 4:18): that alone is the power.

Don't be deceived. There is a place to get where you know the Spirit is upon you, so you will be able to do the works that are performed by this blessed Spirit of God in you, and the manifestation of His power shall be seen, and people will believe in the Lord.

What will make men believe the divine promises of God? Beloved, let me say to you today, God wants you to be ministering spirits, and that means to be clothed with another power. And this divine power, you know when it is there, and you know when it goes forth.

The baptism of Jesus must bring us to have a single eye to the glory of God; everything else is wasted time and wasted energy.

Beloved, we can reach it; it is a high mark, but we can get to it. You ask how? *"Lord, what do You want me to do?"* (Acts 9:6). That is the plan. It means a perfect surrender to the call of God, and perfect obedience.

A dear young Russian came to England. He did not know the language but learned it quickly and was very much used and blessed of God. As the wonderful manifestations of the power of God were seen, the people pressed upon him to know the secret of his power, but he felt it was so secret between him and God that he should not tell it. But they pressed so much that he finally said to them:

> First God called me, and His presence was so precious that I said to God at every call I would obey Him, and I yielded, and yielded, and yielded, until I realized that I was simply clothed with another power altogether, and I realized that God took me, tongue, thoughts, and everything, and I was not myself but it was Christ working through me.

How many of you today have known that God has called you over and over, and has put His hand upon you, but you have not yielded?

How many of you have had the breathing of His power within you, calling you to prayer, and you have to confess you have failed?

"Lord, What Do You Want Me to Do?"

I went to a house one afternoon where I had been called, and met a man at the door. He said, "My wife has not been out of bed for eight months; she is paralyzed. She has been looking so much for you to come; she is hoping God will raise her up."

I went in and rebuked the Devil's power. She said, "I know I am healed. If you go out, I will get up."

I left the house and went away, not hearing anything more about her. I went to a meeting that night, and a man jumped up and said he had something he wanted to say—he had to go to catch a train but wanted to talk first.

He said, "I come to this city once a week, and I visit the sick all over the city. There is a woman I have been visiting, and I was very much distressed about her. She was paralyzed and has lain on that bed many months, but when I went there today she was up doing her work."

I tell this story because I want you to see Jesus.

We had a letter that came to our house that said a young man was very ill. He had been to our mission a few years before with a very bad foot. He had no shoe on, but a piece of leather fastened on the foot. God healed him that day.

Three years later, something else came upon him. What it was, I don't know, but his heart failed, and he was helpless. He could not rise or dress or do anything for himself. In that condition, he called his sister and told her to write to me and see if I would pray.

My wife said to go, and she believed God would give me that life. I went, and when I got to this place, I found the whole county was expecting me. They had said that when I came, this man would be healed.

I said to the woman when I arrived, "I have come."

"Yes," she said, "but it is too late."

"Is he alive?" I asked.

"Yes, just alive," she said.

I went in and put my hands upon him and said, "Martin."

He just breathed slightly and whispered, "The doctor said if I move from this position, I will never move again."

I said, "Do you know the Scripture says, *'God is the strength of my heart and my portion forever'* (Psalm 73:26)?"

He said, "Shall I get up?"

I said, "No."

That day was spent in prayer and ministering the Word. I found a great state of unbelief in that house, but I saw that Martin had faith to be healed. His sister was home from the asylum. God held me there to pray for that place.

I said to the family, "Get Martin's clothes ready, for I believe he is to be raised up." I felt the unbelief.

I went to the chapel and had prayer with a number of people around there, and before noon, they too believed Martin would be healed.

When I returned, I said, "Are his clothes ready?"

They said, "No."

I said, "Oh, will you hinder God's work in this house?"

I went in to Martin's room all alone. I said, "I believe God will do a new thing today. I believe when I lay hands on you, the glory of heaven will fill the place."

I laid my hands on him in the name of the Father, Son, and Holy Spirit, and immediately the glory of the Lord filled the room, and I went headlong to the floor.

I did not see what took place on the bed or in the room, but this young man began to shout out, "Glory, glory!" And I heard him say, "For Thy glory, Lord." And that man stood before me perfectly healed.

He went to the door and opened it, and his father stood there. He said, "Father, the Lord has raised me up," and the father fell to the floor and cried out for salvation.

The young woman brought out of the asylum was perfectly healed at that moment by the power of God in that house.

God wants us to see that the power of God coming upon people has something more in it than we have yet known. The power to heal and to baptize is in this place, but you must say, *"Lord, what do You want me to do?"* (Acts 9:6).

You say it is four months before the harvest. (See John 4:35.) If you had the eyes of Jesus, you would see that the harvest is already here.

The Devil will say you can't have faith; you tell him he is a liar. The Holy Spirit wants you for the purpose of manifesting Jesus through you. Oh, may you never be the same again!

The Holy Spirit moving upon us will make us to be like Him, and we will truly say, *"Lord, what do You want me to do?"*

****

LIFE KEYS FROM THE SERMON

Once again, there is so much for us here, and we need to take it and make it ours. As we explore some of the major points of this message, open your spirit to what God is saying through Wigglesworth, and let these keys bring you to a deeper walk in Christ.

Key #1
OBEDIENCE AND YIELDEDNESS

The place of yieldedness is just where God wants us. People are saying, "I want...I want...I would like to know."...And I see nothing, absolutely nothing in the way except unyieldedness to the plan of God.

God has a plan for your life! You must know this deep in your heart. *"For I know the plans I have for you,' declares the LORD, 'plans to prosper you and not to harm you, plans to give you hope and a future'"* (Jeremiah 29:11 NIV).

God has a plan for your life!

In the archives of heaven there is a blueprint, a plan for your success, drawn before the foundation of the world. If you will yield to God, He will unfold that plan to you and bring it to pass.

> ➢ It is God's will and plan that you be powerfully baptized in the Holy Spirit.
> ➢ It is God's will and plan that you be healed.
> ➢ It is God's will that you have great faith and full assurance of salvation.
> ➢ It is God's will that all the fullness of the abundance of life in the Spirit be yours.

And God's will shall be done, provided your will is not in the way. That is why Jesus would have us pray daily, *"Thy kingdom come. Thy will be done"* (Matthew 6:10 KJV). Unfortunately, our plans are not usually God's plan, and often it will actually block the execution of His plan. This is because our plan is usually based on our own understanding and knowledge.

Before we come to Christ, we are captives of our education and experience. We are products of the twenty, thirty, forty, or more years of the input of life.

When we decide to give our lives to Christ, the journey of transformation begins. We begin to be transformed by the *"renewing of* [our] *mind*[s]*"* (Romans 12:2). Through yielding to God's way and His Word, our thoughts and minds become captive to Christ Jesus, and not captive to the input of life.

> *Bringing every thought into captivity to the obedience of Christ.* (2 Corinthians 10:5)

It is one thing to know the Word, and another thing to be captive to the Word. You are either captive to the world or captive to the Word.

Transformation comes through constantly obeying and constantly yielding. This is the only way. You can go to church all your life; you can spend all your time learning, praying, and singing; but still you will be captive to your past input unless you make the decision to yield and obey every time God shows you something.

Scripture says, *"To obey is better than sacrifice"* (1 Samuel 15:22). If you spend your whole life sacrificing without obeying, sadly, you will never find victory, never find God's plan for you. You may repeatedly sing, "I love you, Lord," but the Word says, *"For this is the love of God, that we keep His commandments"* (1 John 5:3). Through obedience we really demonstrate our love.

Today God will give you an opportunity to go further in obedience. Ask God to show you specifically how you are to obey. Take the opportunity, and you will see the transformation and start to walk in God's plan for your life.

Key #2
SIMPLY BELIEVING

I believe that, after we lay hands on these handkerchiefs and pray over them, they should be handled very sacredly, even as people carry them. They will bring life, if they are carried in faith to a suffering one.

Wigglesworth has been credited with originating the maxim, "God says it, I believe it, and that settles it."[3] Here we find a great example of his complete acceptance of God's truth. He read how the Lord worked through the apostles in the book of Acts, so he simply acted on that Word by doing the same things with unquestioning faith and trust.

He didn't analyze it or intellectually dissect and decipher it. He had learned not to trust in what he knew or thought, but simply to believe what God's Word said. In doing so, he saw thousands of miracles performed around the world through the use of anointed handkerchiefs.

Paul wrote to the Corinthians that he feared that their minds might *"be corrupted from the simplicity that is in Christ"* (2 Corinthians 11:3). The point made by this verse is so important! Simply believe. It is surely a warning for us today, for it is so easy to complicate matters in our present society and lose that simplicity of faith.

With reference to this point, we may note with interest that many more major miracles occur in third-world nations, where the people have hardly been educated, than in the Western world. Several different theories have been put forth about why this is. I believe one of the major reasons is that the people in these nations just simply believe and are healed, while we, in our educated, overintellectual, overanalytical Western world, all too often rationalize away faith for the miraculous.

Jesus said, *"I thank You, Father, Lord of heaven and earth, that You have hidden these things from the wise and prudent and have revealed them to babes"* (Matthew 11:25). So many things are hidden from us through our supposed wisdom and prudence. We must get back to simplicity.

Considered by some to be uneducated and uncouth, Wigglesworth never read any book except the Bible. But one of the reasons for his great faith was this very fact: the Bible was his sole source of knowledge and learning.

During a family discussion, one of my relatives, who is very well read and well educated, expressed concern about how seemingly simple I had become. I had obtained a good education and had always been an avid thinker. In reply to his concern, I found myself saying, "When I surrendered my life to Christ, I gave everything to Him, including my intellect, and I try to simply believe what He says."

Wigglesworth has been credited with originating the maxim, "God says it, I believe it, and that settles it."

Wigglesworth exemplified this reality. He had fully surrendered his thinking and acting in full obedience to God's Word. This is an aspect of his possession by the Spirit of God, and part of the secret of his power.

May God bring us more and more into this same surrender. We must seek God in everything in life. There must come an attitude within us of, "Though I think differently, I will not question your Word. I will simply believe it because You said it. I will not psychoanalyze this situation or give my opinion on it. I will simply believe and obey what You say about it."

After constantly and sincerely doing this for a period of months, a tremendous change in your faith and life will develop. Simply believe.

Key #3
RESEMBLING JESUS

I plead with you in the name of Jesus, especially those of you who are baptized, to awaken to the fact that you have power, if God is with you; but there must be a resemblance between you and Jesus.

"Jesus I know, and Paul I know; but who are you?" Then the man in whom the evil spirit was leaped on them [the seven sons of Sceva], *overpowered them, and prevailed against them, so that they fled out of that house naked and wounded.* (Acts 19:15–16)

You can have a good reputation in your church, you can say all the right words, you can even know all the right phrases and all the right answers, and still be powerless! Powerlessness is the result of your not having the "resemblance of Jesus" in your spirit. The resemblance of Jesus, or Christlikeness, comes through a surrendered life, and it is Christlikeness that brings power in the spirit realm. *"Submit yourselves therefore to God. Resist the devil, and he will flee from you"* (James 4:7 KJV).

When you take authority over the Devil in any situation, what counts is what the Devil sees. If he only sees unsubmitted you, like the seven sons of Sceva, you're in trouble! But if he sees Jesus, he must flee.

The more you yield and are surrendered, the more you are possessed and controlled by the Holy

Spirit, the more you become like Christ, and the more authority Jesus can exert through you in the spiritual realm. The operating principle is:

Obedience brings possession.
Possession brings Christlikeness.
Christlikeness brings power.

This is the secret of Christ. He said,

I can of Myself do nothing. As I hear, I judge; and My judgment is righteous, because I do not seek My own will but the will of the Father who sent Me. (John 5:30)

Jesus was totally yielded and obedient to the Father, and therefore *"God does not give the Spirit by measure* [to Him]*"* (John 3:34). God's Spirit was upon Him without limit, and so He moved in unlimited power. Jesus showed us by His example the way to walk in power.

We can put up a facade in the natural and convince people of our "spirituality." But we cannot fool God, nor can we fool the Devil, no matter what we confess or how loud we shout. The ultimate test is the authority we have in the Spirit.

In actual fact, playing a charade for others destroys faith! Looking for the honor of man and not for the honor of God is the path to religious hypocrisy and powerlessness because it is the antithesis of Christlikeness, and therefore the opposite of "the resemblance of Jesus."

Christ *"made Himself of no reputation"* (Philippians 2:7). *"He* [was] *despised and rejected by men"* (Isaiah 53:3), yet He wielded great spiritual power. Jesus said, in context to this truth:

> *How can you believe, who receive honor from one another, and do not seek the honor that comes from the only God?*   *(John 5:44)*

"How can you believe?" In other words, "How can you have faith in the truth when your behavior reveals that your life is based on falsehood?"

This is the *"having a form of godliness but denying its power"* (2 Timothy 3:5) that the church has become so afflicted with in these last days. We must rid ourselves of this delusion so that we might see the great end-times harvest that God wants to bring on the earth.

Spiritual power comes through faith and humility.

Whenever you realize that you are doing something, anything, to bring the honor of man on yourself—to build your reputation with men or to show your spirituality—you need to stop right there! Ask God's forgiveness and recommit to seeking the *"honor that comes from the only God"* (John 5:44), and seek only to do *"the will of the Father"* (v. 30).

If you do this, you will find so much freedom and such great joy. You will begin to bear the "resemblance of Jesus," and to walk in His authority and power.

Key #4
CLOTHED WITH THE SPIRIT

Do you want power? Don't take it the wrong way. Don't take it as power because you speak in tongues. If God has given you revelations along certain lines, don't take that for the power. Even if you have laid hands on the sick and they have been healed, don't take that for the power. *"The Spirit of the LORD is upon Me"* (Luke 14:18): that alone is the power.

Many Christians are seeking spiritual power today. Praise God for that, for Jesus said, *"Seek, and you will find"* (Matthew 7:7). We so desperately need to see God's power fully operating in this day and age.

[Jesus said,] *He who believes in Me, the works that I do he will do also; and greater works than these he will do, because I go to My Father.*   *(John 14:12)*

Thus we know that *"he who believes"* is meant to move in the same power and do even greater works than Jesus did, but not many are doing so. Why not? Wigglesworth here supplies a key to the answer.

So many men and women are looking in the wrong places. We focus on the latest plan or popular teaching and hope that it will give us power. However, we can't work for it, buy it, or learn it from a book. We fail to realize that it is not the doing that brings power, but the yielding.

We can receive power only as a gift, through yielding and obeying. We may speak in tongues, have great revelations, and even see some healings, but this is far below the pattern we are meant to walk in. God's standard is for us to be fully yielded and controlled, fully possessed, and thus *"clothed with"* (2 Corinthians 5:2) His Spirit and power wherever we go, and in whatever circumstances we find ourselves.

> We can receive God's power only through yielding and obeying.

"The Spirit of the LORD is upon Me" (Luke 4:18) is the true prize that the church is looking for and what God wants to give her. It is the beauty of yielding, the depth of possession, the joy of obedience, and the wonder of His power.

Wigglesworth had it. He lived *"clothed with"* the Spirit, and he continued to talk again and again about it.

If you are finding repetition here, it is so that you might be continually confronted with this model, so that you would adopt this standard as your own, and so that you will not settle for anything less. May you fight and pray, study and yield, until you have it.

This standard is what God wanted to bring the church at the beginning of the twentieth century with the Pentecostal movement beginning at Azusa Street. However, only a few people really seized it for themselves.

In the great last-days harvest that is coming upon the earth, God will establish His standard in the hearts and lives of His people. Many—not just a few, but an army—will walk fully *"clothed with"* (2 Corinthians 5:2) the Holy Spirit. The time is now for the whole body of Christ to be *"clothed with"* the Spirit of Christ.

"The Spirit of the LORD is upon Me." This is true power; this is possession.

Key #5
STEP BY STEP

"First God called me, and His presence was so precious that I said to God at every call I would obey Him, and I yielded, and yielded, and yielded, until I realized that I was simply clothed with another power altogether, and I realized that God took me, tongue, thoughts, and every-thing, and I was not myself but it was Christ working through me."

Only through a process of moment-to-moment yielding do we become completely possessed by the Holy Spirit. Obedience "at every call" is of utmost importance, and God will call daily. When we discover how precious it is to live in obedience, this becomes our delight.

Many Christians think that they are obedient because they do not overtly sin by disobeying the rules—the *do*s and *don't*s. But this is not all there is to it. We must realize that God the Holy Spirit is ever waiting to guide us, to speak to us, to draw us away from the distractions and sinfulness of our sur-roundings just to bring us into fellowship with Him.

When someone comes to Christ, he or she begins to hear God's voice. Romans 8:14 declares, *"For as many as are led by the Spirit of God, these are sons of God."* Sonship is being led by His Spirit. In John 10:4, Jesus said, *"The sheep follow him* [the shepherd], *for they know his voice."* Every day we must listen for His voice and obey as He commands.

Wigglesworth was also influenced by another visiting evangelist who was a very godly man. Though his words were simple, they had a profound effect on those who heard them. The presence of God rested on him to such an extent that people would ask him the secret of his anointing and power. At the Lord's instructions, the minister shared the reason behind His God-given power. He explained,

> "Years ago the Spirit of God began to speak to me, but I was too busy to heed His voice. He persisted, until I commenced to go aside when He spoke, so that I could hear what God the Lord had to say. This became my manner of life. I obeyed His pleading voice; until now, at the slightest breath of the Spirit, I leave everyone and everything to be in His presence, to hear and to obey His Word."[4]

When he heard this testimony and caught the vision of it, Wigglesworth adopted it as a principle by which he would live. Will you appropriate it for your life also?

Each time we hear the voice of the Lord and obey Him, we are further anointed, empowered, consumed, and possessed by the Spirit of God. We must learn to respond every time He calls:

Today, if you will hear His voice, do not
harden your hearts.   *(Hebrews 3:7–8)*

Remain sensitive to His call, and you will grow.
He wants to speak into every area of your life. He
wants to share your joys and your hardships, for He is
your Father. "At every call" you are becoming more
completely *"clothed with"* (2 Corinthians 5:2) the
Spirit of His Son.

Key #6
PRESSING THROUGH

That day was spent in prayer and ministering
the Word. I found a great state of unbelief in
that house, but I saw that Martin had faith to be
healed....I felt the unbelief.

Wigglesworth "felt the unbelief" because it was
so opposed to what he lived in. Wigglesworth lived in
God's presence, in obedience to His voice, and thus
in the realm of faith. So, when he came into an atmosphere that was foreign to this reality, he really
felt it.

When coming across this opposition of faith, this
godless environment, he did not even pretend to have
any quick answers. He knew that he had a fight on
his hands. Because he saw that the one afflicted had
"faith to be healed," he stayed.

Some places exist where we can do nothing because the people are so opposed in spirit and in mind
to God's will through their unbelief. Scripture tells
us that this affected even Jesus: *"Now He did not do*

many mighty works there because of their unbelief" (Matthew 13:58). But Wigglesworth saw some faith here, so he was willing to press through to victory.

We live in an "instant" generation, in a time of quick answers. We have instant coffee, instant dinners, and many things are instantly at hand. We cook our food almost instantly in microwave ovens. Through all this, our patience level has been slowly whittled down.

Spiritually, we have also been affected to the point that we expect immediate, miraculous answers to superficial prayers. Few have any real tenacity these days, any real determination to press through, to "stick it out" until they see the desired result. But patient, enduring faith is what God desires to build in us—the opposite of today's "instant" faith.

Many try "the walk of faith," but because it does not work instantly, they give up and continue in unbelief. Some react by living in a fantasy world of faith clichés, shallow confessions, and vain hopes, never pressing on to real faith.

However, God is looking for a people possessed and controlled by the Spirit, a people who will be led by Him through every situation to enduring and determined faith. This generation, which is to rise up to the call of the last days, needs to be *"rooted and grounded in love"* (Ephesians 3:17) that produces tenacious, lasting faith. The question rings out louder

> We are to be controlled by the Spirit, not by circumstances or unbelief.

than ever before in this instant generation, *"When the Son of Man comes, will he really find faith on the earth?"* (Luke 18:8).

Through hearing from God and obeying His voice, Wigglesworth had learned to press through, to have enduring faith. He spent the whole day in breaking the unbelief, "in prayer and ministering the Word." When he heard from the Spirit of God that faith had been built, assurance came. God gave Him a vision, and the power was released.

Wigglesworth had learned to obey God's Word to the extent that he continued in spiritual warfare until the battle was won and victory was obtained. He did not just come, lay hands on Martin, pray, and say, "Oh well, it didn't work," as many would do, but he pressed through. He didn't just pray once and say, "He's healed," without any assurance in his heart. In situations when he did pray quickly, he had a confidence in his heart from the Lord.

Wigglesworth spoke only when he knew, out of that inward certainty that is faith, that God was about to do something. He pressed through. He persevered. He built the faith level of those around him. Then he watched as God moved.

When you live *"clothed with"* (2 Corinthians 5:2) the Spirit of God and are controlled by Him, you are not controlled by circumstances or unbelief. You may see the circumstances and feel the unbelief, but you are not controlled by them.

God will direct you in each individual situation, as He did Wigglesworth. Are you to pray once and then stand in faith? Should you preach the Word of God first to build faith until assurance comes and then pray? Whatever is needed for the specific circumstance will be revealed to you by the guidance of the Holy Spirit.

This is the way of the *"flame of fire"* (Hebrews 1:7).

Chapter Three

THE BAPTISM IN THE HOLY SPIRIT

PROLOGUE
൶
A Special Train Trip

As the passenger enjoyed the warmth of the morning sun coming through the window, he surmised that the train was making good time. They were already halfway to Cardiff in South Wales. He should have been very content, but this morning was different. Feeling uncomfortable and uneasy, he couldn't understand the sense of guilt that he was experiencing. Memories of things he had done came flooding through his mind, accompanied by an overwhelming sense of fear.

Somehow he knew this had something to do with that man—the older, gray-haired man sitting toward the back corner of the car reading the small book. He tried to divert his focus from him by joining in the conversation and joking with the other passengers, but he just couldn't. His mind kept reverting to that man. Mentally he questioned, "What is it about him? Why, he's a kind old man, with a definite love in his eyes. Why should I fear him?"

The elderly gentleman stood to leave the carriage. The distressed traveler felt a great sense of relief, but that nagging guilt and fear still remained.

Wigglesworth had gone to wash his hands before arriving at his destination. Very aware that the people in his carriage were unsaved, he had been unable to say a word yet, so he continued to pray quietly.

As he walked back along the corridor and entered the carriage, it happened. A wave of guilt and fear enveloped the man sitting by the window as

Wigglesworth walked by him. No longer could the man stand it. He jumped out of his seat, looked straight at Wigglesworth, said, "Sir, you convince me of sin," and sank to his knees.

The same wave swept over the whole carriage as others began saying, "Who are you? You convince us all of sin."

What an opportunity! They all listened, riveted, as this most unusual man explained to them that what they were feeling was the power of God's Holy Spirit convicting them of their sins, that they needed to surrender to Jesus, who would forgive them and wash their sins away.

Real repentance occurred that day, right there in the train carriage. As each one surrendered to Jesus, the guilt and fear left, never to return.[1]

THE BAPTISM IN THE HOLY SPIRIT

Once again, in the prologue to this chapter, we read a remarkable and true testimony of God's grace and power operating through this man. Wigglesworth was in his element. He lived to bring men to his Savior. God flowed through him that day to bring many to Christ.

THE LIFE STANDARD:
Wigglesworth's Middle Years

As we progress in looking at the life and development of Wigglesworth's faith and walk with God, we see that his hunger for more of God led him further and deeper into a search for holiness and the power of the Holy Spirit. Due to that hunger, when he heard in 1907 that people were being baptized in the Holy Spirit and speaking with other tongues as in the book of Acts, he was eager to experience this for himself. Though many people told him it was of the Devil and not of God, his hunger led him straight into what God was doing.

The Holy Spirit was being poured out in an Anglican church in Sunderland, England, under the ministry of the Reverend Alexander Boddy. The first major outpouring of the Holy Spirit in modern times had occurred the year before at Azusa Street in Los Angeles, California. It was spreading to England and other parts of the world.

Shortly after his healing, a man who had been remarkably cured of leg cancer under Wigglesworth's ministry heard about what was occurring in Sunderland. He told Wigglesworth as much as he knew and offered to pay Wigglesworth's expenses should he like to go to find out what was happening.

Wigglesworth was forty-eight years old when he made the journey to Sunderland. This trip would radically alter his life and ultimately change thousands upon thousands of other lives, as God used him to take the message of Pentecost to many nations around the world.

Up to this point, Wigglesworth had experienced several events that had been labeled the baptism in the Holy Spirit. In his early days with the Salvation Army, people would often fall on the ground under God's power during their prayer meetings; sometimes they would be there all night. Some thought that this was the baptism.

Later on, after a ten-day fast, Wigglesworth experienced a level of blessing and sanctification that had a profound effect on his life. He was delivered of a previously unmanageable temper, and afterwards he was able to speak a little more freely. At the time, he considered this to be the baptism in the Holy Spirit. In fact, he believed that he had been baptized in the Spirit right up until the time he went to Sunderland, telling those in the meetings so.

Even with this preconception, Wigglesworth's intense hunger drove him on, seeking for more. He disturbed many of the meetings because he spoke out what was on his mind, sometimes very bluntly. Many of the people there rebuked him for this.

A missionary from India especially criticized him for spoiling their meetings. Wigglesworth, trying to justify himself, ended up in a very unpleasant discussion with the missionary. However, God brought them together the following night. Wigglesworth had misplaced his key and was locked out of his room. Spending the night together in the missionary's room, the two men prayed as God led them. As they interceded through the night, a mighty blessing and anointing filled their room.

For four days, Wigglesworth sought God intensely in prayer, wanting "nothing but God." Though the power and blessing of God were upon him, Wigglesworth still hadn't received what those at the "seeking" meetings talked about. He decided it was time to go home. In the course of leaving, he dropped by the vicarage to say good-bye. Mrs. Boddy, the pastor's wife, told him boldly that he needed the baptism in the Holy Spirit despite what he thought, and she proceeded to lay hands on him in prayer.

Shortly afterwards, Mrs. Boddy left the room to answer a knock at the door, and the fire of God fell. Wigglesworth was bathed in a glorious power and received a consciousness that he was cleansed by the blood of Jesus. So real was this consciousness that he cried out, "Clean, clean, clean! Hallelujah!"

He had received his Pentecost. But this wasn't all! Filled with joy, he had a vision of the empty cross and of Jesus Christ, exalted at the right hand of the Father. Finally, praise in an unknown language started flowing from his lips—he was speaking in *"other tongues, as the Spirit gave* [him] *utterance"* (Acts 2:4).[2]

Wigglesworth's hunger had at last won through all his preconceptions, through all that was thought about him, and through the rebukes he had received. Spiritual hunger is the driving factor, the force that will carry us through all opposition. It is the characteristic that makes a man or woman stand out in the kingdom of God.

Some of those who had rebuked Wigglesworth had been seeking and waiting for the baptism for months, but they had not received. When they heard that this disruptive man had received it after only a few days, they became very discontented. God used Wigglesworth even in his own baptism *"to provoke them to jealousy* [and]...*to emulation"* (Romans 11:11, 14 KJV). A new hunger came into the meetings in Sunderland from that day. In a short period, fifty of them received the Holy Spirit baptism.[3]

The message those people had read on his life was that of hunger—hunger for all that God could give. They thought that they were seeking until he came, disrupted their peaceful meetings, and showed them what seeking really was.

We in the body of Christ need to cultivate a hunger in our hearts as this man Wigglesworth did, not allowing it to be quenched. We must allow it to grow until it takes over the whole of our lives, breaking through our preconceptions and misconceptions, our religious ideas and teachings, our own thoughts and experiences. Then we will see the new realms and the higher ground that God is calling us to.

We need the baptism in the Holy Spirit—a radical baptism in the Holy Spirit. But let's not stop there. Wigglesworth used to say that he would rather have a man on the platform with him that was not baptized in the Holy Spirit, yet

> **We need to cultivate a hunger for God.**

was hungry for God, than a man who was baptized but had become satisfied with his experience.

So many today are satisfied with their present level of experience. If you are one, I hope that as you see Wigglesworth's life, you will come into great dissatisfaction with your current position. I hope you will be left with a continual longing to live ever as *"a flame of fire"* (Hebrews 1:7).

****

The Baptism in the Holy Spirit
A Message by Smith Wigglesworth

For John truly baptized with water, but you shall be baptized with the Holy Spirit not many days from now....But you shall receive power when the Holy Spirit has come upon you; and you shall be witnesses to Me in Jerusalem, and in all Judea and Samaria, and to the end of the earth.
—Acts 1:5, 8

Beloved, the Lord would have us know in these days that there is a fullness of God where all other powers must cease to be. I beseech you this afternoon to know that the baptism in the Holy Spirit is to possess us so that we are to be continually full of His utterances and revelations and divine perception, so that we may be so remarkably controlled by the Spirit of God that we live and move in a glorious sphere of usefulness for His glory.

If we will read John's gospel, we will see that Jesus predicted all that we are getting today in the Holy Spirit. He said that the Holy Spirit would talk of the things of His Word and reveal them unto us. He would live out in us all the life of the Lord Jesus Christ.

If we could only think what this really means! Talk about graduation of the Holy Spirit, and you will simply outstrip everything they have in any college in the land. You would leave that which is as cold as ice and move out into the sunshine. God the Holy Spirit desires us to have such a fullness of the Spirit that we shall not be ignorant, neither will we have mystic conceptions, but we will have a clear, unmistakable revelation of all the mind of God for these days.

I beseech you, beloved, in the name of Jesus, that you might see that you must come right into all the mind of God. Jesus truly said, *"But you shall receive power when the Holy Spirit has come upon you"* (Acts 1:8).

I want you to know that *"He...presented Himself alive after His suffering by many infallible proofs, being seen by them during forty days and speaking of the things pertaining to the kingdom of God"* (Acts 1:3). He is all the time unfolding to every one of us the power of His resurrection.

Remember, the baptism in the Holy Spirit is resurrection. If you can touch this ideal with its resurrection power, you will see that nothing earthly can remain. You will see that disease cannot remain. If you get filled with the Holy Spirit, all your physical afflictions, including all the nervous, fearful conditions, must go. Resurrection is to breathe in you Christ's life and to cause you to know that you are quickened by the Spirit in the life of Jesus.

Oh, the word *resurrection!* I wish I could say it just on parallel lines with the name *Jesus.* They very harmoniously go together. Jesus is resurrection, and to know Jesus in this resurrection power is simply to see that you are no more to be dead, but *"alive to God"* (Romans 6:11) by the Spirit.

We must see that we are no good unless God takes charge of us. But when He gets total control of us, what a plan for our lives! What a wonderful open door for God!

Oh, brethren, we must see this ideal by the Spirit! What shall we do? Do? You dare not do anything but "go through." Submit to the power of God. If you yield, other people are saved.

When you know the power of resurrection, other people will be raised out of death and be taken out of all kinds of evil into a blessed life through the Spirit. Beloved, we must see that this baptism of the Spirit is greater than all.

Remember, when I talk about resurrection, I talk about one of the greatest things in the Scriptures, because resurrection is an evidence that we have wakened to a new revelation of truth that cannot cease to be, but will always go on with greater force and increasing power with God.

See to it that this day makes you press on with a new order of the Spirit, so that you can never be where you were before. This is a new day for us all. You say, "What about the people who are already baptized?" Oh, this is a new day also for those who have been baptized, for the Spirit is an unlimited source of power.

There is nothing stationary in God. God has no place for a man who is stationary. The man who is going to catch the fire, hold for the truth, always be on the watchtower, is the man who is going to be a beacon for all saints, having a light greater than his natural order.

I must see that God's grace and God's life and His Spirit are mightier than man a million times. When you are baptized in the Holy Spirit, you are on an extraordinary plane. You are brought into line with the mind of God. If you want the quickening that moves your body until you know you are renewed, it is in the Holy Spirit.

And while I say so much about the Holy Spirit today, I withdraw everything that does not put our Lord Jesus Christ in the place He belongs, for when I speak about the Holy Spirit, it is always with reference to the revelation of Jesus. The Holy Spirit is simply the

Revealer of the mighty Christ who has all for us, so that we may never know any weakness, but all limitations are gone. Glory to God!

The Holy Spirit never comes until there is a place ready for Him. The Holy Spirit can only come into our bodies, His temples, when they are fully yielded to Him. It does not matter what kind of a building you get: the building cannot be a substitute for the temple of the Holy Spirit. You will have to be Holy Spirit temples to have the building anything like the Holy Spirit order.

On the Day of Pentecost, the Holy Spirit could not come until the apostles and those who were with them in the Upper Room were all of one mind and one heart, all of *"one accord"* (Acts 1:14) with each other and with God.

You will notice that Jesus said, *"I thank You, Father, Lord of heaven and earth, that You have hidden these things from the wise and prudent and have revealed them to babes"* (Matthew 11:25). This is the mind and plan of God for all who desire to seek the Holy Spirit.

What is the difference between the wise, prudent man and a baby? If you have the "babe spirit" this afternoon and will yield to God and let Him have His way, He will fill you with the Holy Spirit. The natural man cannot receive the Spirit of God, but when you get into a supernatural place, then you will receive the mind of God.

Oh, beloved, if we can only be *"babes"* today, great things will take place in the thought of the Spirit of

God. The Lord wants us all to be so in like-mindedness with Him that He can put His seal on us.

****

LIFE KEYS FROM THE SERMON

Key #1
UTTERANCES, REVELATIONS, AND PERCEPTIONS

Know that the baptism in the Holy Spirit is to possess us so that we are to be continually full of His utterances and revelations and divine perception, so that we may be so remarkably controlled by the Spirit of God that we live and move in a glorious sphere of usefulness for His glory.

To "live and move in a glorious sphere of usefulness for His glory" is God's purpose for every one of us. Again, this only comes as the Spirit gains possession of us.

As we lay down our lives daily and say, *"Not* [my] *will, but Yours, be done"* (Luke 22:42), as the prayer *"Thy kingdom come. Thy will be done"* (Matthew 6:10 KJV) becomes the focal point of our existence, as we continue to hunger for God's plan to be worked out in our lives, then everything gives way to the Holy Spirit. He begins to take charge of our thoughts, our emotions, and our bodies.

Remember, this is always voluntary, never forced, and does not come to anyone who does not want it.

94

However, the one who wants to be really used of God, to "live...in a glorious sphere of usefulness for His glory," must come into this reality.

This is when we begin to speak in "His utterances," to understand by His "revelations," and to see with "divine perception." Our words have little effect in comparison to His utterances. Our understanding cannot stand in the light of His revelations. We will not see with accurate perspectives until we begin to see with divine perceptions. This is why we need to be controlled by His Spirit.

Wigglesworth alludes to his belief that there are different degrees of the baptism in the Holy Spirit. As we hunger for God and surrender to His will, we add fuel to the fire of our baptism in the Holy Spirit, until it becomes a mighty, mighty blaze. This is what we need.

When Scripture tells us to *"be filled with the Spirit"* (Ephesians 5:18), the word *"filled"* is in the present-continuous tense, meaning "continually filled." So it becomes, *"be* [continually] *filled with the Spirit."* What Wigglesworth is trying to develop in our hearts is a greater hunger to be further filled and never to stop desiring more until we are "remarkably controlled."

Key #2
RESURRECTION POWER

Remember, the baptism in the Holy Spirit is resurrection. If you can touch this ideal with its resurrection power, you will see that nothing earthly can remain.

Wigglesworth would often say in his meetings, "I am one hundred percent Pentecostal." That he was. The baptism in the Holy Spirit was vital and priceless to him. When the baptism was again poured out at the beginning of the 1900s after centuries of obscurity, it seemed to be far more treasured and appreciated than it is today. Wigglesworth valued it dearly. Throughout his preaching, the baptism was a constant theme to a deeper life in Christ.

The Holy Spirit comes to bring revelation of Christ, and through that revelation brings us into the power of the Christ-life. This is the "resurrection power" we need. I believe we must take a fresh look at the baptism in the Holy Spirit and rediscover a true appreciation of its great value.

> ➢ It is resurrection! But too many settle for less than resurrection power.
> ➢ It is resurrection! But too many are still living in the death of sin.
> ➢ It is where nothing earthly can remain! But too many live with so much that is earthly in their lives.

The standard of life God has for us in Christ Jesus is nothing less than resurrection life. Jesus said, *"I am the resurrection and the life"* (John 11:25). He did not say, "I going to tell you or teach you about the resurrection and the life." Rather, He said, *"I am the resurrection and the life."*

As the baptism in the Holy Spirit is to set up Jesus as King, it is also to set up resurrection and life as the ruling factor in the whole being—spirit, soul, and body.

These days, we have shifted our emphasis from entering deeper and deeper into the Spirit to seeking God's life and power through learning and knowledge. But the life is in the Spirit. The Holy Spirit is calling for saints to put down their books and magazines, turn off their television sets, and spend more time in the Spirit:

➢ In intercession: Wigglesworth said that he never went half an hour without praying.
➢ In praying in the Spirit: Wigglesworth constantly prayed in the Holy Spirit, for the "gift of tongues" was a priceless treasure to him.
➢ In worshiping: worship was another great love of Wigglesworth. He would get caught up in it, both dancing and singing in the Spirit.
➢ In meditating on the Word: Wigglesworth read the Word at every meal, and read and meditated upon it whenever he had a spare moment. "Some like to read their Bible in Hebrew. Some...in Greek. I prefer to read mine in the Holy Ghost!"[4]
➢ In fellowshipping with God: Wigglesworth, through daily doing all these things faithfully over a period of time, learned to walk in virtually unbroken fellowship with God.

Our goal must become unbroken fellowship with God, which is the highest honor and reward given to man. In doing these things, we continue to deepen our Holy Spirit baptism, and we further our walk in the fullness of resurrection life.

Key #3
HIS PLAN

But when He gets total control of us, what a plan for our lives! What a wonderful open door for God!

Oh, brethren, we must see this ideal by the Spirit! What shall we do? Do? You dare not do anything but "go through." Submit to the power of God. If you yield, other people are saved.

The book of Revelation gives us a picture of Jesus as *"He who opens and no one shuts, and shuts and no one opens,"* who says, *"I know your works. See, I have set before you an open door, and no one can shut it"* (Revelation 3:7–8).

Every day, He has a new door for us to go through, a further yielding and a further fulfilling of His plan in our lives. The plan is not completely in effect until we are fully yielded and He is in control. The power cannot flow unrestrictedly through us until we are operating fully in that plan.

Praise God for the understanding He gave Wigglesworth! We live in a day when there are so many evangelism seminars, courses, plans, and programs. Unfortunately, some have learned all about evangelism techniques, yet they do not see significant results in winning souls to Christ.

Intricate, in-depth methodologies are at our fingertips, yet Wigglesworth just says that if you yield, other people will be saved! What audacity! How dare this uneducated English plumber make it so simple!

Seriously, however, the power on Smith Wigglesworth to win souls was so phenomenal that he really did have more authority than most others to speak on the subject.

Incidents such as the example related at the beginning of this chapter about the conversion of many on the train illustrate this power in his life. In his eighties, after he had suffered a stroke, he would frequently go to the local park that was close to his home in Bradford, since he was not traveling or preaching at this time. Such was the power of evangelism on his life that while he was just sitting on a park bench, people would be drawn to him. Every day he had the privilege to lead several to Christ, as well as to pray for others for deliverance and healing.

> If you yield to God, others will be saved.

This reality at work in his life gave him the authority to speak as he did. He said that if you yield to the Lord, others will be saved. Again, we come back to the major theme of his life and message—yieldedness and obedience. If we are going to be effective evangelists and ultimately see the revival we long for, this is the most powerful and most needed teaching in the church in these last days.

Do you really desire the people around you to be saved? Then apply this Wigglesworth key in your life. As you seek God for His plan, and obey it, others around you will be converted.

What is God speaking to you at this time? What is your conscience disturbing you about? What is that thing you have been meaning to deal with in your life? What truth keeps standing out to you as you read the Word of God? What direction has God given you that you haven't yet followed? What new door has opened for you?

If you will yield and obey step by step, if you will go through the doors He opens before you, if you will let Him have entire control of you, then you will see God's power manifested in your life, and others around you will meet the Lord.

Key #4
KNOW THE REVEALER

And while I say so much about the Holy Spirit today, I withdraw everything that does not put our Lord Jesus Christ in the place He belongs, for when I speak about the Holy Spirit, it is always with reference to the revelation of Jesus.

Being possessed by the Holy Spirit is being surrendered to the Revealer of Christ. It is to be totally consumed with the revelation of Christ—His life, His death, His resurrection, His position, His authority, His power, His compassion, His mind, His desire— all that He is.

An unbreakable link exists between a relationship with the Holy Spirit and knowing Christ. Many seek Christ through knowledge about Him without building a relationship with the Holy Spirit, and they end up confused and unbalanced in their perceptions of Jesus. Even theologians who have written volumes on the Bible may be in this group. Of course, personal intimacy with Christ comes from the Word of God, but it comes through the Word being imparted to us by the Holy Spirit.

Wigglesworth's life was such a great example of this impartation of the Word by the Holy Spirit that many well-educated Bible scholars were astonished at the great revelation he had. The only book he ever read was the Bible, but he

> By living in the Holy Spirit realm, we can develop deep intimacy with God.

had never received any formal education. He was taught solely by Holy Spirit revelation.

Jesus made an astounding statement when He said,

It is to your advantage that I go away; for if I do not go away, the Helper will not come to you; but if I depart, I will send Him to you.
(John 16:7)

Here Jesus was talking to men who, for three years, had lived with Him every day, heard Him, watched Him, and seen all His miracles. They had actually walked with the Son of God.

I have often dreamed of what it would have been like to have lived at that time. Early in my Christian walk, I asked God why I couldn't have been born in that day. God answered me by showing me the remarkable truth of this Scripture.

Jesus said that it is actually better for us that He went away! How could this be? He knew there was a new reality, a new realm coming where we could all know Him better, draw closer to Him, and have a much deeper relationship with Him than the disciples had even when they were living and walking with Him for three years in Israel! This new reality was the coming of the Holy Spirit, the Comforter, the Helper, the Spirit of Truth, who is to *"teach* [us] *all things"* (John 14:26).

Wigglesworth came to have such a deep revelation of Christ and such an intimacy with God by yielding to this new reality of living in the Holy Spirit realm. My friend, you too can know Jesus more intimately through the Holy Spirit than if you had been one of Christ's companions when He walked as a man here on earth!

We all need to enhance and develop our relationship with the Holy Spirit, for through Him we know Christ. We also need to appreciate and fully cherish the baptism in the Holy Spirit.

The fact is that you can have the standard of the baptism that Wigglesworth had, because *"God shows no partiality"* (Acts 10:34). The question is, do you want it? And second, will you develop it?

Key #5
PREPARING THE PLACE

The Holy Spirit never comes until there is a place ready for Him. The Holy Spirit can only come into our bodies, His temples, when they are fully yielded to Him....

On the Day of Pentecost, the Holy Spirit could not come until the apostles and those who were with them in the Upper Room were all of one mind and one heart, all of *"one accord"* (Acts 1:14) with each other and with God.

Another major part of deepening your relationship with the Holy Spirit and receiving the constant infilling is preparing the place within yourself and keeping it prepared. Constant preparation means constant infilling.

Wigglesworth's preaching was continually aimed at getting people into the practice of preparation—to the place where they are fully yielded to Him. Once again, the secret is yielding. Yielding is surrender; yielding is obedience; yielding is death to self; yielding is holiness and purity.

Twelve months after his baptism in the Spirit, Wigglesworth wrote, in a letter about receiving the fullness of the Holy Spirit, "The filthy acts of the self-life have to be dealt with, and men cannot always stand the purging."[5] Dealing with sin and self is necessary in preparing the place because the Holy Spirit is just that—the *Holy* Spirit.

The other part of preparing the place Wigglesworth talks about here is unity—one mind, one heart, one accord with God and with others. Unity can come only as we are humble before God and man, for when we are seeking our own glory and not God's, we cannot be in full accord with Him or His body, the church.

Before we can see the great move of God that He desires to bring to the whole earth, churches and individuals need to put away their arguing and division, humble themselves, join hands and hearts, and seek only the glory of God. Where there is no unity, there is no real Holy Spirit power.

You may think you have a "great anointing," but if you are living in self and sin, you need to rethink that. We pass many things off as anointing that are actually just natural God-given gifts.

Incredibly, people can continue to see results in their ministries by the gifts in their lives, even though they have fallen back into a sinful lifestyle and are seeking their own glory. This is only because of God's grace, for the Word says, *"The gifts and the calling of God are irrevocable"* (Romans 11:29).

However, even with manifested results, such people are living very dangerously and won't last long in the ministry. These are "flash in the pan" ministries, the "shooting stars." Leaders of such ministries draw people to themselves for a season, but their ministries do not stand the test of time, for they are not yielded to the Spirit of God, but only to self and sin.

Because the "Wigglesworth epistle" speaks of the persistent faithfulness, holiness, and humility that characterized his life, it is so valuable to us. The twentieth century saw some great evangelists who shone for a season, but, due to a lack of these qualities or a lack of depth in them, tragically fell. Whether it be "the girls, the gold, or the glory," a man's *"sin will find* [him] *out"* (Numbers 32:23).

We need people with Holy Spirit anointing, not just natural gifts.

What we really need in the body of Christ today is enduring ministries and ministers built on solid "Holy Spirit anointing," and not just on giftings. We need holy people. *"One accord"* (Acts 1:14) people. "Flames of fire" under His control, yielded and humble. Men and women who live in the prepared place.

Key #6
THE "BABE SPIRIT"

Jesus said, *"I thank You, Father, Lord of heaven and earth, that You have hidden these things from the wise and prudent and have revealed them to babes"* (Matthew 11:25). This is the mind and plan of God for all who desire to seek the Holy Spirit....If you have the "babe spirit" this afternoon and will yield to God and let Him have His way, He will fill you with the Holy Spirit.

How beautiful it is to have the "babe spirit," the ultimate place of yielding, the prepared place.

Unless you are converted and become as little children, you will by no means enter the kingdom of heaven. Therefore whoever humbles himself as this little child is the greatest in the kingdom of heaven. (Matthew 18:3–4)

We must humble ourselves. It's our job. We all must decide to become like little children, to have a "babe spirit."

A child is totally dependent: we must decide to be so. A child is unknowing but has an inward drive to learn: with all our knowledge, we still know very little of real godly truth. But as we acknowledge this to God and to ourselves, the drive to learn God's way will come. A child is pure, innocent, and without conceit: this is the prepared place. A child is totally trusting of his or her parents. Can we become like little children to the point where we totally, unquestioningly, unthinkingly trust God in everything? The return to these wonderful attributes of the child brings revelation, brings the power and the anointing, and prepares the place for further possession.

Become childlike before the Lord and find true spiritual maturity.

In the quest for Christian maturity, many have made the mistake of correlating it to natural maturity and have lost the "babe spirit." Christian maturity is the total opposite of the world's view. Natural maturity is when a man or woman becomes independent, but spiritual maturity is when we become totally dependent on God.

Life in Christ, in so many ways, is a paradox. The way up is down. The greatest is he who serves. The way to receive is to give. The way to find your life is to lose it.

When believers lose the "babe spirit," they lose their openness, teachableness, dependence, excitement, and humility, and they ultimately move out of God's plans for their lives. My friend, if you have lost the "babe spirit," you need to repent and humble yourself. Become a child once again before the Lord. It really is worth it.

Chapter Four

"THAT I MAY KNOW HIM"

PROLOGUE
✂
"Raise Your Finger"

She lay motionless on the bed. The very scent of death seemed to fill the room. For many months, the tumor had sapped away both her life and her will to live. Once, all she had wanted was to live for her children, but the pain had become unbearable. Now it seemed that there was no hope.

Awakened early by the excruciating throbbing that racked her entire body, she now lay praying against her old familiar enemy. She had nothing else left. No longer did she have the strength to move or cry out even if she desired to. Even though she believed that she could be healed, she couldn't help thinking that this day would be her last. Life could have been so wonderful, but life like this wasn't worth living. A loud knock at the door interrupted her thoughts.

Mr. Fisher, an elder from her church, quietly announced, "I've brought someone to see you. This is Mr. Wigglesworth. He's going to pray for you."

Out of the corner of her eye, she caught a glimpse of him, an older man with a gray mustache and a twinkle in his eye. A definite air of authority was about him as he spoke. She sensed his love of Jesus.

"I know you are very weak, but if you wish to be healed and cannot lift your arm, or move it at all, it might be possible that you can raise your finger."

Something about this man, the strange air of authority, even the tone of his voice, seemed to spark faith in her. "Yes, yes I do want to be healed! I must let him know," tumbled through her mind.

With every bit of strength she could muster, she concentrated on raising her index finger. As the men stared intently, they almost missed the slight shift.

Suddenly everything changed. The pain had vanished. She wasn't in her bedroom anymore, but was surrounded by countless numbers of people and such glorious singing.

And there was Jesus. Oh, how lovely He is, she thought. His face shone with a light that lit up everything.

"She's dead. She's dead." Mr. Fisher was panic-stricken, his face contorted with fear. He had brought Wigglesworth, hoping that she might be healed, and now she had died. What would people think? Would they believe that it was his fault? He slumped in a chair with his face in his hands, moaning, "Oh, what shall I do?"

While Mr. Fisher groaned, Wigglesworth tossed back the covers, reached into the bed, and pulled her out. Carrying her lifeless body across the room, he propped it up against the wall. There was no pulse, no breath. She was absolutely dead.

He looked into her face, and sternly he commanded: "In the name of Jesus, I rebuke this death." Mr. Fisher looked up in amazement. Was he absurd? What was he doing? Before he could say a word, her whole body began to tremble.

"In the name of Jesus, I command you to walk." All she knew was that Jesus looked directly at her and pointed. Oh, what a beautiful time she'd been having, but as Jesus looked at her, she knew she had to go back for the children. Jesus faded from view as she suddenly heard, "In the name of Jesus, in the name of Jesus, walk!"

She awoke to find herself walking across her bedroom floor. She felt so strong and alive! The pain was gone, the tumor had disappeared. Mr. Fisher stood with his mouth wide open, just staring at her.

That night her astonished doctor sat in the congregation as she told her remarkable story. She would never forget her visit to heaven, or her visit from the man with the twinkle in his eye and the faith in his words, Smith Wigglesworth.[1]

"THAT I MAY KNOW HIM"

T he heartfelt cry of the apostle Paul in Philippians 3:10 was, *"That I may know Him."* Certainly, the cry of Smith Wigglesworth's heart echoed Paul's.

Perhaps the greatest culmination of this desire was his hunger for the Word of God, of which he ate daily for many years of his life. His communion with God was totally centered around the Word, so much so that he literally became "a man of one book"—the great Book, the Bible. Reportedly, it was the only book he ever read.

His constant companion, the Word was continually in his hand, even in times of relaxation. Instead of reading newspapers or magazines as others would when traveling, he read his Bible. His son-in-law James Salter, who knew him very well and traveled many years with him, said, "He never considered himself fully dressed without a copy of the Word of God in his pocket."[2]

> Wigglesworth "never considered himself fully dressed without a copy of the Word in his pocket."

Because he worked twelve to sixteen hours a day from the tender age of seven to help support his family, Wigglesworth was robbed of a basic education and was functionally illiterate. Even so, in his teen years he always carried a New Testament with him wherever he went. Although he couldn't read much, he had a tremendous appreciation and respect for the Bible, even at this young age.

Wigglesworth did not learn to read properly until he was in his mid-twenties, when his new wife Polly taught him to read from the Bible and to write. From that time, the Bible became his great love.

So vital did he consider the reading of the Word that he insisted on reading a chapter at every meal. This came from the revelation that the need for nourishment spiritually was more important than the physical need for food.

Many people know that Scripture says, *"Man shall not live by bread alone, but by every word of God"* (Luke 4:4), but how many of us live in this reality and eat the Word as we eat food? Wigglesworth did. He literally considered the "eating" of the Word of God of as much or more importance than eating food. Thus, he made it his habit to read a chapter whenever or wherever he sat down to eat.

Once, when staying in Israel in a missionary home managed by a lady known for the strictness of her time schedule, he sat down for dinner and began as usual to read from the Scriptures. His hostess asked him to stop as it didn't fit in with the time allotted for the meal. Firmly, but respectfully, Wigglesworth insisted that to hear from the Father was a vitally essential part of the meal. Seeing the great authority and conviction with which he shared this, she conceded. It was said that the whole atmosphere of the house changed from then on.

> LIFE KEY: Here is a practical key from Wigglesworth's life that you need to act on. At every meal, read a Scripture passage. If you are with others, read it aloud and discuss it for a few minutes during the meal.

How Wigglesworth loved the Word. He considered it the most precious thing in all the world. He would say that if he could not get another copy, he would not give his Bible away for anything in the world. He even made a challenge that "he would give a five-pound reward to anyone who could catch him, at any time, without either his Bible or his Testament."[3] Five pounds was a considerable amount of money in those days.

He knew that he could only know and understand God by the Word—not by his feelings or experiences—so he sought God continually in His Word. Wigglesworth had learned the secret of drawing away from everything to go and be with God. To be shut in with God and His Word became his constant habit. Thus, Wigglesworth didn't just acquire knowledge, but came to know the Living Word. He grew to have "a consuming love for the Word of God" and "an overwhelming confidence in the God of the Word."[4]

In this present day, many people amass intellectual knowledge of the Word but do not deeply love it.

The Bible tells us that knowledge gained without love *"puffs up, but love edifies* [builds up]*"* (1 Corinthians 8:1). It is the *"faith working through love"* (Galatians 5:6) by which we are edified, and by which Wigglesworth's faith was built.

As well as reading the Word, he constantly stimulated others to do the same, inspiring them to emulate his same love and commitment to it. He encouraged young and old alike to read it, memorize it, and hide it in their hearts so they could use it all the time. He often declared as he preached:

The Bible is the Word of God:

> supernatural in origin,
> eternal in duration,
> inexpressible in value,
> infinite in scope,
> regenerative in power,
> infallible in authority,
> universal in interest,
> personal in application,
> inspired in totality.

Read it through, write it down, pray it in, work it out, and then pass it on.

Truly the Word of God changes a man until he becomes an "epistle of God." It transforms his mind, changes his character, moves him on from grace to grace, and makes him an inheritor of the very nature of God. God comes in, dwells in, walks in, talks through, and sups with him who opens his being to the Word of God.[5]

In addition, he taught that the Word was to be fully and implicitly obeyed, quoting the Scripture, *"Behold, to obey is better than sacrifice"* (1 Samuel 15:22). Obey he did, and he expected others to obey also. He knew that obedience was the normal response of real faith. Out of this obedience and reliance on the Word, his ministry grew.

He became so impregnated with the Word that when he preached, it flowed from the depths of his inner man and brought a tremendous consciousness of the reality of God to both believers and nonbelievers. Because such an incredible volume of God's Word had saturated his soul and spirit, a great, great faith was built in him. It was said that he would literally "inoculate" his audiences with the same faith—faith to be healed, faith to be delivered, faith to receive a miracle. And signs, wonders, and miracles flowed like rivers in his meetings.

> The Word flowed from the depths of Wigglesworth's inner man, and signs, wonders, and miracles flowed like rivers in his meetings.

He changed the atmosphere wherever he went, bringing conviction to unbelievers and to believers alike. He brought faith, hunger, and a great sweetness of the Holy Spirit. Of course, we know that it was not him, but the Living Word that was in him.

No one will deny that today we need to see the kind of miracles and power that were manifested in Smith Wigglesworth's ministry. We see here, written on the epistle of his life, another key to that miracle power. Anyone who will love and cherish the Word of God, making it his daily food and his priceless treasure, is on the right path to power, authority, and Christlikeness.

You have probably heard before of the necessity of reading the Word, and you will hear it again. However, only when you take it to your heart and are consumed by an overpowering love for God's Word, as this man was, will you ever begin to realize God's full plan for your life.

I cannot stress enough the importance of this page of the Wigglesworth epistle. Hunger is the driving force of the walk of power. But the Word is its solid foundation, the rock on which the house is built. *"For no other foundation can anyone lay than that which is laid, which is Jesus Christ"* (1 Corinthians 3:11). Jesus is the Word.

May God raise up a generation whose love for Him rules their time schedules, rather than their time schedules ruling their love for Him; who will count spiritual food more important than physical food and eat it as their great delight; who will walk continually in power and not just hope that the power will come someday; who will let the living Word, Jesus Christ, possess their lives and change their world; and who will never stop crying, *"That I may know Him"* (Philippians 3:10).

****

"That I May Know Him"
A Message by Smith Wigglesworth

I believe the Lord would be pleased for us to read from the third chapter of Philippians this morning:

> *For we are the circumcision, who worship God in the Spirit, rejoice in Christ Jesus, and have no confidence in the flesh....But what things were gain to me, these I have counted loss for Christ. Yet indeed I also count all things loss for the excellence of the knowledge of Christ Jesus my Lord, for whom I have suffered the loss of all things, and count them as rubbish, that I may gain Christ and be found in Him, not having my own righteousness, which is from the law, but that which is through faith in Christ, the righteousness which is from God by faith; that I may know Him and the power of His resurrection, and the fellowship of His sufferings, being conformed to His death, if, by any means, I may attain to the resurrection from the dead. Not that I have already attained, or am already perfected; but I press on, that I may lay hold of that for which Christ Jesus has also laid hold of me. Brethren, I do not count myself to have apprehended; but one thing I do, forgetting those things which are behind and reaching forward to those things which are ahead, I press toward the goal for the prize of the upward call of God in Christ Jesus.* (Philippians 3:3, 7–14)

One can only pray for God to enlarge these visions today. I believe that God will, by His power, bring us into like-minded precious faith to believe all the Scriptures say.

The Scriptures are at such depths that one can never be able to enter into those things without being enlarged in God. Beloved, one thing is certain this morning: God can do it.

"All things that pertain to life and godliness" (2 Peter 1:3) are in reach with a faith that will not have a dim view, but clears away everything and claims all that God puts before it. So this morning, I pray God to so unfold to us the depths of His righteousness that we may no longer be poor, but very rich in God by His Spirit. Beloved, it is God's thought to make us all very rich in grace and in the knowledge of God through our Lord Jesus Christ.

We have before us this morning a message that is full of heights, and depths, and lengths, and breadths — a message that came out of brokenness of spirit, the loss of all things, enduring all things, a message where flesh and all that pertains to this world had to come to nothing.

We can never worship God, except in the Spirit. God can take us into this spiritual plane with Himself so that we may be grounded in all knowledge, so settled on all spiritual lines until, from that place, we will always be lifted by God.

Men try to lift themselves, but there is no inspiration in that. But when you are lifted by the Spirit, when you are taken on with God, things all come into perfect harmony, and you go forth right on to victory. That is a grand place to come to, where we *"rejoice in Christ Jesus, and have no confidence in the flesh"* (Philippians 3:3).

Paul added, *"Though I also might have confidence in the flesh"* (v. 4). Paul had kept the law blamelessly, but I find that Another held him in the same place. Oh, that is the greatest of all, when the Lord Jesus has the reins. Then we no longer have anything to boast about, because we see all our perfection according to law-keeping, and law-abiding ceases.

Oh, it is beautiful as we gaze upon the perfect Jesus! Jesus so outstrips everything else. For this reason, Paul felt that everything must become as dross—whatever he was, whatever he had been. There was no help for anything in him. There is no help for us, only on the lines of helplessness and nothingness.

I know nothing like a travail in the Spirit. Oh, it is a burden until you are relieved. I have had those days, and I have had it this morning, but now God is lifting.

And I say, brother, sister, unless God brings us into a place of brokenness of spirit, unless God remolds us in the great plan of His will for us, the best of us shall utterly fail. But when we are absolutely taken in hand by the almighty God, God makes even weakness strength. He makes even that barren, helpless, groaning cry come forth so that men and women are born in the travail.

There is a place where the helplessness is touched by the almightiness of God, and where you come out shining as gold tried in the fire.

Oh, beloved, I see there is hope for Pentecost only on broken conditions. It was there on the cross that our Lord died with a broken heart. Pentecost came out of jeering and sneering, a sip of vinegar, a smite with a rod, a judgment that was passed away from Him, and a cross that he had to bear.

But glory to God! Pentecost rings out this morning through the Word. *"It is finished"* (John 19:30) for you! Now, because it is finished, we can take the same place that He took and rise out of that death in majestic glory with the resurrection touch of heaven that will make people know from today that God has done something for us.

Every day there must be a revival touch in our hearts. Every day must change us after His fashion. We are to be made new all the time. There is no such thing as having all grace and knowledge. There is a beginning, and God would have us begin in all these beatitudes of power this morning, and never cease but rise and rise and go on to perfection. There are some beatitudes here that God must have us reach this day!

> *But what things were gain to me, these I have counted loss for Christ. Yet indeed I also count all things loss for the excellence of the knowledge of Christ Jesus my Lord, for whom I have suffered the loss of all things, and count them as rubbish, that I may gain Christ.* (Philippians 3:7–8)

Also, we will turn to Hebrews 10:32:

> *But recall the former days in which, after you were illuminated, you endured a great struggle with sufferings.*

I am positive that no man can attain like-mindedness on these lines except by the illumination of the Spirit.

God has been speaking to me over and over again that I must press all the people to receive the baptism of the Holy Spirit, because I see in the baptism of the Holy Spirit unlimited grace and the endurance in that revelation by the Spirit.

I see that the excellency of Christ can never be understood except by illumination. And I find the Holy Spirit is that great Illuminator who makes me understand all the depths of Him. I must witness Christ. Jesus said to Thomas, *"Thomas, because you have seen Me, you have believed. Blessed are those who have not seen and yet have believed"* (John 20:29).

So I can see there is a revelation that brings me into touch with Him where we get all and see right into the fullness of our Head, even Christ. And I can see how Paul, as he saw the depths and heights of the grandeur, longed that he might gain Him.

Before his conversion, in his passion and zeal, Paul would do anything to bring Christians to death. And that passion that was in him raged like a mighty lion. As he was going on the way to Damascus, he heard the voice of Jesus saying, *"Saul, Saul, why are you persecuting Me?"* (Acts 9:4).

What broke him was the tenderness of God. Brother, it is always God's tenderness over our weakness and over our depravity that has broken us all the time. If someone came along to thwart us, we would stand in our corner, but when we come to One who forgives us all, we do not know what to do. Oh, to win Him, beloved!

There are a thousand things in the nucleus of a human heart that need softening a thousand times a day. There are things in us that, unless God shows us the excellence of the knowledge of Him, will never be broken and brought to ashes. But God will do it. Not merely to be saved, but to be saved a thousand times over!

Oh, this transforming regeneration by the power of the Spirit of the living God makes me see there is a place to win Him, that I may stand complete there. As He was, so am I to be. The Scriptures declare it shall be:

> *And be found in Him, not having my own right-eousness, which is from the law, but that which is through faith in Christ, the righteousness which is from God by faith.* (Philippians 3:9)

How glorious not to depend on my works but upon the faithfulness of God, being able under all circumstances to be hidden in Him, covered by the almighty presence of God!

The Scriptures declare that we are in Christ, and Christ is in God. What is able to move you from that place of omnipotent power? *"Shall tribulation, or distress, or persecution, or famine, or nakedness, or peril, or sword?"* (Romans 8:35). Ah, no! Shall death, or life, or principalities, or powers (v. 38)? *"Yet in all these things we are more than conquerors through Him who loved us"* (v. 37). But we must be *"found in Him"*! There is a place of seclusion, a place of rest and faith in Jesus where there is nothing else like it.

When Jesus came on the water to the disciples, they were terrified, but He said, *"It is I; do not be afraid"* (Matthew 14:27). Beloved, He is always there. He is there in the storm as well as in the peace; He is there in the adversity. When shall we know He is there? When we are *"found in Him"* (Philippians 3:9), not having our own work or our own plans, but resting in the omnipotent plan of God.

Oh, is it possible for the child of God to fail? No. *"Behold, He who keeps Israel shall neither slumber nor sleep"* (Psalm 121:4). He shall watch over us continually, but we must be *"found in Him."*

I know there is a covert place in Jesus that opens to us this morning. Brethren, you have been nearly weighed down with troubles. They have almost crushed you. Sometimes you thought you would never get out of this place of difficulty. But you have no idea that behind the whole thing, God has been working a plan greater than all. *"That I may know Him and the power of His resurrection"* (Philippians 3:10).

Jesus said to Martha, *"I am the resurrection and the life"* (John 11:25). Today is a resurrection day. We must know the resurrection of His power in brokenness of spirit. Oh, to know this power of resurrection, to know the rest of faith! To know the supplanting of His power in you this morning! To make you see that any one of us, without exception, can reach these beatitudes in the Spirit.

Ah, there is something different between saying you have faith and then being pressed into a tight corner and proving you have faith. If you dare to believe, it shall be done *"according to your faith"* (Matthew 9:29). *"Whatever things you ask when you pray, believe that you receive them, and you will have them"* (Mark 11:24).

Jesus is the resurrection and the life, and I say we must attain to it. God help us to attain. We attain to it in the knowledge that He who came forth will make us *"white as snow"* (Isaiah 1:18), pure and holy as He, so that we may go with boldness to the throne of grace (Hebrews 4:16).

Boldness is in His holiness. Boldness is in His righteousness. Boldness is in His truth. You cannot have the boldness of faith if you are not pure.

What a blessed word follows: *"The fellowship of His sufferings"* (Philippians 3:10). Remember, unless that fellowship touches us, we shall never have much power. What helped Him at all times—when He saw the withered hand, when He saw the woman bowed over who in no way could help herself? When the Spirit of the Lord blows upon you, you will be broken down and then built up.

Jesus came forth in the glory of the Father, filled with all the fullness of God. It was the thought of God before the foundation of the world, with such love over all the fearful, helpless human race, with all its blackness and hideousness of sin. And God loved, and God brought redemption.

"That I May Know Him"

May God give us this morning such *"fellowship of His sufferings"* (Philippians 3:10) that, when we see the person afflicted with cancer, we will pray right through until the roots are struck dead. When we see the crooked and helpless woman or man, so infirm, may God give us a compassion, may God give us a fellowship with them that shall undo their heavy burdens and set them free.

How often we have missed the victory because we did not have the Lord's compassion at the needed moment. We failed to go through with a broken heart.

Is there anything more? Oh yes, we must see the next thing.

Being conformed to His death.   *(Philippians 3:10)*

Unless a grain of wheat falls into the ground and dies, it remains alone; but if it dies, it produces much grain.   *(John 12:24)*

God wants you to see that unless you are dead indeed, unless you come into a perfect crucifixion, unless you die with Him, you are not in *"the fellowship of His sufferings."* May God move upon us in this life to bring us into an absolute death, not merely to talk about it, but a death through which His life may indeed be manifest. Paul said,

I do not count myself to have apprehended; but one thing I do, forgetting those things which are behind and reaching forward to those things which are ahead, I press toward the goal for the prize of the upward call of God in Christ Jesus.   *(Philippians 3:13–14)*

He had just said that he was following after in order to apprehend that for which he had been apprehended by Christ Jesus. And I believe God wants us to come this morning in like-mindedness, so that we may be able to say, "I know I am apprehended." The Lord wants us to understand that we must come to a place where our natural lives cease and, by the power of God, we rise into lives where God rules, where He reigns.

Do you long to know Him? Do you long to be *"found in Him"* (Philippians 3:9)? Your longing shall be satisfied this day. This is a day of putting on and being *"clothed with"* (2 Corinthians 5:2) God. All you who want to know God, yield to His mighty power and obey the Spirit.

****

LIFE KEYS FROM THE SERMON

Key #1
THE SPIRIT, NOT THE FLESH

Men try to lift themselves, but there is no inspiration in that. But when you are lifted by the Spirit, when you are taken on with God, things all come into perfect harmony, and you go forth right on to victory.

To be lifted by the Spirit is our objective. If we are lifted by the beauty of the singing, the special effects and lighting, the grandeur of the choir, the enthusiasm of the preacher, but not by the Spirit of God, we have missed it. "Men try to lift themselves, but there is no inspiration in that."

We can leave a meeting inspired, having been pumped up in our souls (our minds and emotions). Unfortunately, if this is all that has happened, the next day there will be no change in our lives.

However, if we are lifted by the Spirit, the inspiration will last, and real spiritual growth will occur. How many people leave church services on Sunday elevated and entertained, but the rest of the week live in defeat, not victory?

The true test, the "litmus paper," of your church attendance, is this: first, does it produce fruit in your life; and second, is it taking you on with God and into victory?

If you answered in the negative to these questions, you have two alternatives to consider: either something is wrong with you, and you need to repent and surrender to the Holy Spirit, or something is wrong with the church you are attending, and you need to go where the Spirit of God is moving. Either way, you need to get on your knees, pray, and seek God earnestly and honestly until you know which it is. Otherwise, you are living in spiritual death!

> If we are lifted by the Spirit, the inspiration will last.

But I do mean pray! Don't go church-hopping, as so many people are prone to do, when the changes are needed within you and not in the church. Equally, do not stay in a "spiritual mausoleum," or even a vibrantly exciting yet "soulish" church, if God shows you that it is hindering your growth.

"Men try to lift themselves, but there is no inspiration in that." Wigglesworth was truly a man of the Spirit. He wouldn't tolerate preachers vaunting their own personalities and not the person of the Holy Spirit, or pumping things up by their own abilities or natural charisma. In fact, he dealt severely with those who did so, even on the platform in major conventions.

May God keep us ministers from falling into, or continuing in, this trap. Preachers, *"today, if you will hear His voice, do not harden your hearts"* (Hebrews 3:7–8). I know this is an easy trap to fall prey to, for I have done it often.

Too many showmen exist in the church today; don't be another one. A gifted man can easily elicit a good response from a congregation or take a sizeable offering. But for God to really move and produce lasting changes in lives, the minister and those ministered to must pay the price and be "lifted by the Spirit."

Key #2
BROKENNESS

And I say, brother, sister, unless God brings us into a place of brokenness of spirit, unless God remolds us in the great plan of His will for us, the best of us shall utterly fail....

Oh, beloved, I see there is hope for Pentecost only on broken conditions.

Brokenness is the key, for *"You do not delight in burnt offering. The sacrifices of God are a broken spirit, a broken and a contrite heart; these, O God, You will not despise"* (Psalm 51:16–17).

Our burnt offerings, in this day, are our trying to "lift ourselves," but the key to being lifted by the Spirit and walking in victory is this very *"broken and...contrite heart"* that God speaks about in the book of Psalms.

Wigglesworth would also say that deep faith comes only from brokenness, for faith is the basis of Pentecost. Much has been lost in the Pentecostal movement because of the lack of the preaching of this truth. Too many people these days want their *"itching ears"* (2 Timothy 4:3) tickled. They want to hear the easy way, the "latest revelation," and this truth is neither easy nor popular. Unfortunately, many have become like the Greeks at Athens in Acts 17:21 who *"spent their time in nothing else but either to tell or to hear some new thing."* Yet Wigglesworth saw very clearly that "there is hope for Pentecost only on broken conditions."

The Bible says, *"We are His workmanship"* (Ephesians 2:10). As such, we need remolding. However, before we can be reshaped, certain things have to be broken: our own abilities, our own ideas, our own ways—in fact, everything that is our own and not His own.

Wigglesworth knew the process, for he was a broken man. He would say,

> It seems to me as if I had had a thousand road engines come over my life to break me up like

a potter's vessel. There is no way into the deep things of God but by a broken spirit. There is no other way into the power of God.[6]

If we are to attain to the standard of faith and Holy Spirit power that this man had, we must grasp this concept and allow God to bring us into brokenness. Just as at the Last Supper Jesus took the bread, blessed it, broke it, and then gave it to His disciples, so also, if we are to be the bread of life to this dying generation, He must also take us, bless us, and break us. Then He can give of Himself through us, as He did through Wigglesworth to multitudes around the world.

> **We are to be the bread of life to this dying generation.**

There are a thousand things in the nucleus of a human heart that need softening a thousand times a day. There are things in us that, unless God shows us the excellence of the knowledge of Him, will never be broken and brought to ashes. But God will do it. Not merely to be saved, but to be saved a thousand times over!

If Jesus is to be King, then all that is not of Jesus must be broken and brought to ashes. So many things are not of Him, so many things in our hearts are the counterfeit of the Spirit of Christ, because they were established there by the spirit of the world. All these must go, for we are being *"conformed to the image of His Son"* (Romans 8:29). As God shows us *"the excellence of the knowledge of [Him]"* (Phil. 3:8), and we set our hearts and minds on it, things start to break, our hearts are softened, and the *"refiner's fire"* (Malachi 3:2) burns away whatever is not of Him.

As we continue day by day to look into *"the excellence of the knowledge of* [Him]," we continue to be molded. *"Looking unto Jesus, the author and finisher of our faith"* (Hebrews 12:2). "What you see is what you get," or rather, what you put before you and continually look upon is what you become like. And just as "there are a thousand things in the nucleus of a human heart that need softening a thousand times a day," we need to look to Jesus a thousand times a day, into *"the excellence of the knowledge of* [Him]."

Wigglesworth would cry, "Oh, what a lovely Jesus!" Through the softening and breaking process in his life, he looked to Jesus, and Jesus became "a lovely Jesus."

Key #3
"FOUND IN HIM"

When shall we know He is there? When we are *"found in Him"* (Philippians 3:9), not having our own work or our own plans, but resting in the omnipotent plan of God.

He who abides in Me, and I in him, bears much fruit; for without Me you can do nothing.
(John 15:5)

To abide in Christ, to be *"found in Him,"* what an incredible reality! This is our goal, our purpose, and God's ultimate purpose for us. Abiding in Him is the other side of being possessed by the Spirit of God, the fruit of brokenness, and the beauty of the Christ-life. When He truly reigns as King in us in all things, then we will always be *"found in Him."*

Paul talked about being *"found in Him"* in Philippians 3:9, and he went on to say in verse 12, *"Not that I have already attained,...but I press on."* Scripture tells us that we are already in Christ, but Paul was going a step further by talking about the full appropriation of this reality in his life. He "pressed on" with all his heart, and so must we.

One of Wigglesworth's constant themes is the hidden life, a life *"hidden with Christ."* *"For you died, and your life is hidden with Christ in God"* (Colossians 3:3). It is a life in *"the secret place of the Most High"* (Psalm 91:1), so that we might say with the psalmist, *"You are my hiding place"* (Psalm 32:7).

When we live fully in His plan and not our plans, His ideas and not our ideas, His thoughts and not our thoughts (see Isaiah 55:8–9), His work and not our own, then our lives are hidden in Christ because we have reached the point of brokenness. You must find this place if you really want to be used of God. When you do, you will really know that He is there.

Every day must be a step toward living in this place, being *"found in Him,"* where your mind stops and His mind begins to take over, where your thoughts cease and He fills you with His thoughts. Your devotional time is not just an opportunity to give God your list of requests, but rather a time of change and trans-formation, a time of surrender and becoming one with God. Each day, set yourself a specific time of total sur-render, of seeking God to take over your thoughts, plans, dreams, visions, feelings—in short, everything.

This is yielding; this is possession. You must know, though, that God will not take over your will and force you into this place. You never lose your will. Possession is when your will is daily given to Him so that you may enter *"the secret place"* and be *"found in Him."*

Key #4
BOLDNESS

Boldness is in His holiness. Boldness is in His righteousness. Boldness is in His truth. You cannot have the boldness of faith if you are not pure.

> *And be found in Him, not having my own righteousness, which is from the law, but that which is through faith in Christ, the right-eousness which is from God by faith.*
> *(Philippians 3:9)*

As we increasingly *"gain Christ"* (v. 8) and are *"found in Him,"* the more we come into real right-eousness, or right standing with God. As we grow in His righteousness, we grow in the boldness of faith, because the two are inseparably linked.

Isaiah 64:6 says, *"Our righteousnesses are like filthy rags."* Yet Proverbs 28:1 states that *"the righteous are bold as a lion."* In these verses we see two different types of righteousness: self-righteousness, trying to obtain right standing with God by our own deeds; and God's right-eousness, resting in the right standing that Jesus won for us. We may think we are living in God's right-eousness without realizing that we are still operating in our own. God's righteousness will produce purity, holiness, and the boldness of faith. Our righteousness absolutely will not.

> God's righteousness must become our greatest quest if we really want the boldness of faith.

Are you living in purity? Are you living in holiness? Do you keep trying to be pure and holy, but never seem to get there? If so, then you need to *"hunger and thirst for* [His] *righteousness"* (Matthew 5:6) until you are filled. All your efforts to be righteous in your own strength will fail.

His righteousness must become our greatest quest if we really want the boldness of faith. We must be consumed with passion to *"be found in Him, not having* [our] *own righteousness"* (Philippians 3:9).

Have you ever wondered about truly great men and women of faith and how they obtained such a distinction? They share the same secret for acquiring great faith: they have gone continually to the *"secret place"* (Psalm 91:1) and found His holiness, His righteousness, and His truth, until they have been *"found in Him"* broken, purified, and bold in faith.

Key #5
The Fellowship of His Sufferings

Remember, unless that fellowship touches us, we shall never have much power....

May God give us this morning such *"fellowship of His sufferings"* (Philippians 3:10) that, when we see the person afflicted with cancer, we will pray right through until the roots are struck dead. When we see the crooked and helpless woman or man, so infirm, may God give us a compassion, may God give us a fellowship with them that shall undo their heavy burdens and set them free.

How often we have missed the victory because we did not have the Lord's compassion at the needed moment. We failed to go through with a broken heart.

Oh, my brother and sister, please catch this vital key. Wigglesworth had this great compassion, the compassion of Jesus, which must become ours. This *"fellowship of His sufferings"* brings the urgency, endurance, and empathy to our prayers, so that we will pray through until we obtain victory. Lacking this, we are likely just to pray once and then give up.

We see here an element of faith that cannot come from promotional jargon and positive thinking, but comes only from a broken heart. Wigglesworth would weep as he ministered to the sick. Unless you come to the place where you are compelled to do the same, you will not see many healed. This truth is a missing ingredient in much of today's popular teaching, yet it is vital to the faith God wants us to have for the great end-times harvest.

My friend, do not resist the breaking of the Lord. Allow His hand to break and remold you until you are soft, pliable, and filled with compassion for others. If compassion is lacking in your life, you need to yearn with Paul to *"know...the fellowship of His sufferings"* (Philippians 3:10). You need to return repeatedly to Calvary to see Jesus and become consumed with the wonder of the awesome sacrifice of His death—how He bore all sin, all sickness, all sorrow and death. Then go down to an inner-city mission or hospital, or somewhere that hurt and sickness and despair reign, until you feel what He felt for them, until your heart breaks as His did, until your greatest longing is to lay down your life for them as His was.

> Let's not miss the victory because we lack the Lord's compassion.

Let's not miss the victory because we lack the Lord's compassion. Let's not miss the blessedness of being *"moved with compassion"* (Mark 1:41) as Jesus was because we have failed to be *"conformed to His death"* (Philippians 3:10).

Key #6
"CONFORMED TO HIS DEATH"

The Lord wants us to understand that we must come to a place where our natural lives cease, and by the power of God we rise into lives where God rules, where He reigns.

"That I May Know Him"

Do you long to know Him? Do you long to be *"found in Him"* (Philippians 3:9)?

He who finds his life will lose it, and he who loses his life for My sake will find it.
(Matthew 10:39)

Your life is no good! Get rid of it! The natural life—your life—must cease. Only when your life ceases can His life truly begin in you. Only then does He have room to live through you without you getting in the way.

What a blessed reality! A literal loathing of our fleshly lives—our thoughts, our plans, our dreams, our works, and all our ways—must grow within us until we know that all of self leads to death.

If we fail to lose our lives willingly in the present and allow the Lord to replace His life for ours, then we will lose our lives at the hand of death when there will be no replacement. If we do not loathe it, we will not lose it.

Jesus said, *"If anyone comes to Me and does not* **hate**...*his own life also, he cannot be My disciple"* (Luke 14:26, emphasis added). Deal with it totally, and you will have fullness of life in Christ; compromise with it, and you will just get by. He wants your whole life.

The key here is loathing and longing. Loathe the old, where self rules. Long for the new, where God rules and reigns, and where all the ingredients of the life, nature, and character of Christ are shining and operating in you. Now that's life!

Chapter Five

"COUNT IT ALL JOY"

PROLOGUE

❈

"Good-bye, Polly"

"Smith, watch me when I'm preaching. I get so near to heaven when I'm preaching that some day I'll be off."

He thought back on these words that his dear Polly had once spoken. "Well," he mused, "she certainly must have preached tonight."

It was New Year's Day, 1913. The local doctor and a policeman had met him just as he was stepping out the front door, on his way to Glasgow to minister at some meetings. However, the look on the two men's faces as they met him told him that something was wrong.

"Polly's dead, Smith. She fell dead at the mission door." Just a few hours before, he had bid her well as she was leaving to go preach there.

How he loved his Polly. She was everything in the world to him. In the natural he was devastated, but deep down inside, he knew that she was where she wanted to be. He began to speak in tongues and praise the Lord, laughing in the Spirit.

Soon the house was filled with people. Her body had been brought to the house. At Wigglesworth's instructions, they took her up to her room and laid her lifeless form on the bed.

"She's dead, and we can do no more." Wigglesworth just smiled. He knew differently.

Asking everyone to please leave the room, he closed the door when the last one had left. He turned around and walked over to her bed. He knew that she was with her beloved Lord as she had so longed to be, but standing before her now, he couldn't bear the separation.

"In the name of Jesus, death give her up." Polly's eyes opened and looked straight into his. "Polly, I need you."

"Smith, the Lord wants me."

An incredible struggle was going on inside him now. Oh, how much he wanted her with him. How could he go on without her? He had thought that they would have so many more years together.

That still, small voice came—the voice he knew so well, the only one he loved more than hers. "She's mine. Her work is done."

With tears streaming down his face, he yielded to his Lord. "My darling, if the Lord wants you, I will not hold you."

She smiled as he kissed her cheek tenderly. Then he simply said, "Good-bye for the present." Her eyes closed, and she was gone.

"Yes, Lord." He had obeyed. He turned and walked out of the room. It was the hardest thing he had ever done.[1]

"Count It All Joy"

H ow do we obtain great faith?" is a question often asked, but given so many varied answers. I believe it is best answered by someone who has known great faith, who has shown the fruits of great faith. Smith Wigglesworth was such a man, so much so that he was called "The Apostle of Faith."

The Life Standard:
Wigglesworth's Middle Years (Cont.)

Through faith, Wigglesworth led tens of thousands around the world to Christ. Through faith, tens of thousands were healed under his hands and ministry: the deaf heard, the blind saw, the crippled walked, those with cancer were completely delivered and lived long lives. Through faith, he raised fourteen people from the dead, including his own wife, Polly, and saw multitudes raised up from their sickbeds.

Jesus said, *"You will know them by their fruits"* (Matthew 7:16). Wigglesworth certainly had tremendous fruit—fruit that is still reproducing today. This is surely a man of whom we can ask the question,

"How do we obtain great faith?" and receive an authoritative answer.

Wigglesworth repeatedly quoted Mark 4:28 to explain how faith grows: *"First the blade, then the ear, after that the full corn in the ear"* (KJV). His constant answer to the question about obtaining faith was,

> Great faith is the product of great fights. Great testimonies are the outcome of great tests. Great triumphs can only come out of great trials. Every stumbling block must become a stepping stone, and every opposition must become an opportunity.[2]

Here we see another of the keys to his life, his faith, and his ministry, because these weren't just mere words. Rather, he spoke from a lifetime of experience.

His desire was to be transformed into the image of his Lord. People who knew him have told me that this was the obvious and remarkable reality of his life: he was totally consumed with pleasing Jesus and becoming like Him.

He would often cry out during meetings, "Filled with God, filled with God, emptied of self, and filled with God."[3] This was the longing of his heart. But this filling does not come easily, and the one who reaches out for it comes to know trials and hardships

> **Wigglesworth was consumed with pleasing Jesus and becoming like Him.**

as companions. Wigglesworth stretched for it with a tenacity that would not allow any manner of trial, hardship, or any other thing stop his pursuit.

The great faith that God gave to Smith Wigglesworth truly came from great "fights of faith." God tells us through Paul to *"fight the good fight of faith"* (1 Timothy 6:12). Although at times the fight seemed hard and painful, it was always good. Wigglesworth fought many and varied "good fights" in his life. Knowing that they were for his own growth and *"more precious than gold"* (1 Peter 1:7), he learned to *"count it all joy"* (James 1:2). He would sing,

> Make me better, make me purer,
> By the fire which refines,
> Where the breath of God is sweeter,
> Where the brightest glory shines.

In January 1913, the news came to him that Polly, his wife, had died. She was only fifty-one years old. How hard it was for this man who had loved his wife so very deeply to let her go. He said of her, "All that I am today I owe, under God, to my precious wife. Oh, she was lovely!"[4]

To carry on without her was for him tremendously hard and a "great fight." He was to live on earth and minister for another thirty-four years without her, but he did not question the Lord.

He later said that this was his "greatest and costliest test of obedience."[5] One evening, in New Zealand, after a great series of meetings, his host asked him about the secret of his power and success. With tears in his eyes, he answered,

I am sorry you asked me that question, but I will answer it.

I am a brokenhearted man. My wife, who meant everything to me, died eleven years ago. After the funeral, I went back and lay on her grave. I wanted to die there. But God spoke to me and told me to rise up and come away. I told Him if He would give me a double portion of the Spirit—my wife's and my own—I would go and preach the Gospel.

God was gracious to me and answered my request. But I sail the high seas alone. I am a lonely man, and many a time all I can do is to weep and weep.[6]

Almost two years following Polly's death, George, their youngest son, died. Wigglesworth said while preaching,

It seems to me as if I had had a thousand road engines come over my life to break me up like a potter's vessel. There is no other way into the deep things of God but a broken spirit.[7]

As we have seen, he wasn't just speaking shallow words here. He was a broken man, yet he would say, "The best thing that you ever could have is a great trial. It is your 'robing time.' It is your coming into inheritance. Voice your position in God and you will be surrounded by all the resources of God in the time of trial."[8]

Truly surrendered, this man had great faith. While in his seventies, Wigglesworth was to go through a trial that showed his tremendous tenacity and perseverance of faith, a trial that very few of us could endure. The only reason he did endure it was because of the faith that the Lord had developed in his life through having fought and won so many previous battles.

In this last full decade of his life, he was given the diagnosis that he had kidney stones in an advanced stage, a very serious condition. He was also told that he should have an operation to save him from this long and painful illness that would eventually take his life.

He replied to all of this by saying, "Doctor, the God who made this body is the one who can cure it. No knife shall ever cut it so long as I live."[9]

He was a man who meant what he said. He let his "'Yes,' be 'Yes,' and [his] 'No,' 'No,'" (James 5:12). For six years, he stuck by his word. At times he passed so much blood as the kidney stones came through his system that his cheeks turned ashen, and he would have to be wrapped in heavy rugs to keep him warm. At night he would roll on the floor in agony, yet he continued to conduct two or three meetings a day, sometimes attending to thousands at a time, ministering healing and deliverance to the sick around the globe.

> In his seventies, Wigglesworth went through a painful trial that showed his tremendous tenacity and perseverance of faith.

Though this pain is beyond imagining, his ministry and his faith did not change. He continued with unquenchable zeal, with fiery preaching, and with deep compassion for the sick. Wigglesworth passed hundreds of kidney stones during those six years, yet he never wavered in his resolution to trust God completely for his total restoration.

His son-in-law, James Salter, said of this time,

> One cannot find the answer to the struggle of those days and years in the iron constitution and will of steel, both of which he possessed; for I have seen those things break down under lesser tests. He did not just bear those agonies; he made them serve the purpose of God and gloried in and over them.[10]

How remarkable!

When he passed the last of the stones, he emerged with a faith tried by fire, greater and stronger than ever. He became "more than a conqueror" (see Romans 8:37), for he was set on glorifying God in everything and not compromising in anything.

This level of faith and dedication is available to anyone who is prepared to give all to Christ and to be totally consumed by His love—to anyone who will, in every situation and every trial, in every test and every fight, *"count it all joy"* (James 1:2).

****

Count It All Joy
A Message by Smith Wigglesworth

My brethren, count it all joy
when you fall into various trials.
—James 1:2

"Count It All Joy"

This letter was addressed *"to the twelve tribes which are scattered abroad"* (James 1:1). Only one like the Master could stand and say to the people *"count it all joy"* when they were scattered everywhere, driven to their wits' end, and persecuted. The Scriptures say that *"they wandered in deserts and mountains, in dens and caves of the earth"* (Hebrews 11:38).

These people were scattered abroad, but God was with them. It does not matter where you are if God is with you. He who is for you is a million times more than all that can be against you. Oh, if we could, by the grace of God, see that the beatitudes of God's divine power come to us with such divine sweetness, whispering to us, "Be still, my child. All is well." Only be still and see the salvation of the Lord.

Oh, what would happen if we learned the secret to ask only once and believe? What an advantage it would be if we could just come to a place where we know that everything is within reach of us. God wants us to see that every obstacle can be moved away.

God brings us into a place where the difficulties are, where the pressure is, where the hard corner is, where everything is so difficult that you know there are no possibilities on the human side—God must do it.

All these places are of God's ordering. God allows trials, difficulties, temptations, and perplexities to come right along our path, but there is not a temptation or trial that can come to man for which God does not have a way out. You do not have the way out, but it is God who can bring you through.

A lot of saints come to me and want me to pray for their nervous systems. I guarantee there is not a person in the whole world who could be nervous if they understood 1 John 4. Let us read verses 16 to 18:

> *And we have known and believed the love that God has for us. God is love, and he who abides in love abides in God, and God in him. Love has been perfected among us in this: that we may have boldness in the day of judgment; because as He is, so are we in this world. There is no fear in love; but perfect love casts out fear, because fear involves torment. But he who fears has not been made perfect in love.*
> *(1 John 4:16–18)*

Let me tell you what perfect love is: *"He who overcomes the world...believes that Jesus is the Son of God"* (1 John 5:5).

What is the evidence and assurance of salvation? He who believes on the Lord Jesus in his heart. Every expression of love is in the heart. When you begin to breathe out your heart to God in affection, the very being of you, the whole self of you, desires Him.

Perfect love means that Jesus has got a grip on your intentions, desires, and thoughts, and has purified everything. Perfect love cannot fear.

What God wants is to impregnate us with His Word. His Word is a living truth. I would pity one who has gone a whole week without temptation. Why? Because God only tries the people who are worthy. If you are passing through difficulties, and trials are rising, and darkness is appearing, and everything becomes so dense that you cannot see through, hallelujah! God is seeing through.

He is a God of deliverance, a God of power. Oh, He is near to you if you will only believe. He can anoint you with fresh oil; He can make your cup run over. Jesus is the Balm of Gilead and, yes, the Rose of Sharon.

I believe that God the Holy Spirit wants to bring us into line with such perfection of beatitude, of beauty, that we shall say, *"Though He slay me, yet will I trust Him"* (Job 13:15). When the hand of God is upon you and the clay is fresh in the Potter's hand, the vessel will be made perfect as you are made pliable in the almightiness of God.

Only melted gold is minted; only moistened clay is molded; only softened wax receives the seal; only broken and contrite hearts receive the mark as the Potter turns us on His wheel, shaped and burned to take and keep the mark, the mold, the stamp of God's pure gold.

He can put the stamp on you this morning. He can mold you afresh. He can change the vision. He can move the difficulty. The Lord of Hosts is in the midst of you and is waiting for your affection.

Remember this question, *"Simon, son of Jonah, do you love Me more than these?"* (John 21:15).

He never lets the chastening rod fall upon anything except that which is marring the vessel. If there is anything in you that is not yielded and bent to the plan of the Almighty, you cannot preserve that which is only spiritual in part.

When the Spirit of the Lord gets perfect control, then we begin to be *"changed...from glory to glory"* (2 Corinthians 3:18) by the expression of God's light in our human frame, and the whole of the body begins to have the fullness of His life manifested until God so has us that we believe all things.

Brother, sister, if God brings you into oneness and the fellowship with the most high God, your nature will quiver in His presence. But God can chase away all the unrest, all the unfaithfulness, all the defects, all the wavering, and He can establish you with such strong consolation of almightiness that you just rest there in the Holy Spirit by the power of God, ready to be revealed. God invites us to higher heights and deeper depths.

> Make me better, make me purer,
> By the fire which refines,
> Where the breath of God is sweeter,
> Where the brightest glory shines.
>
> Bring me higher up the mountain
> Into fellowship with Thee,
> In Thy light I'll see the fountain
> And the blood that cleanseth me.

I am realizing very truly these days that there is a sanctification of the Spirit where the thoughts are holy, where the life is beautiful with no blemish. As you come closer into the presence of God, the Spirit wafts revelations of His holiness until He shows us a new plan for the present and the future.

The heights and the depths, the breadths and the lengths of God's inheritance for us are truly wonderful. We read in Romans 8:10, *"And if Christ is in you, the body is dead because of sin, but the Spirit is life because of righteousness."*

Oh, what a vision, beloved! *"The body is dead"* because sin is being judged, is being destroyed. The whole body is absolutely put to death, and because of that position, there is His righteousness, His beauty; and the *"Spirit is life,"* freedom, joy.

The Spirit lifts the soul into the presence of heaven. Ah, this is glorious.

"Count it all joy when you fall into various trials" (James 1:2). Perhaps you have been counting it all sadness until now. Never mind; you turn the scale, and you will get a lot more out of it, more than you ever had before. Tell it to Jesus now. Express your inward heartthrobbings to Him.

> He knows it all, He knows it all,
> My Father knows, He knows it all.
> The bitter tears, how fast they fall,
> He knows, my Father knows it all.

Sometimes I change the words. And I would like to sing to you these changes because there are two sides to it:

> The joy He gives that overflows,
> He knows, my Father knows it all.

Ah, yes, the bitterness may come at night, but the joy will come in the morning, hallelujah (Psalm 30:5)! So many believers never look up. *"Jesus lifted up His eyes and said, 'Father, I thank You that You have heard me'"* (John 11:41). *"He cried with a loud voice, 'Lazarus, come forth!'"* (John 11:43).

Beloved, God wants us to have a resurrection touch about us. We may enter into things that will bring us sorrow and trouble, but through them God will bring us to a deeper knowledge of Himself.

Never use your human plan when God speaks His Word. You have your cue from an almighty Source that has all the resources, that never fades away.

His wealth is past measuring, abounding with extravagances of abundance, waiting to be poured out on us. Hear what the Scripture says: *"God...gives to all liberally and without reproach"* (James 1:5).

The almighty hand of God comes to our weakness and says, "If you dare to trust Me and will not waver, I will abundantly satisfy you out of the treasure-house of the Most High."

"And without reproach." What does this mean? He forgives, He supplies, He opens the door into His fullness and makes us know that He has done it all. When you come to Him again, He gives you another overflow without measure, an expression of a Father's love.

Who wants anything from God? He can satisfy every need. He satisfies *"the hungry with good things"* (Luke 1:53).

I believe that a real weeping would be good for us. You are in a poor way if you cannot weep. I do thank God for my tears. They help me so that I do like to weep in the presence of God.

I ask you in the name of Jesus, will you cast all your care on Him? *"For He cares for you"* (1 Peter 5:7).

I am in great need this morning; I do want an overflow. Come on, beloved, let us weep together. God will help us. Glory to God. How He meets the need of the hungry.

****

LIFE KEYS FROM THE SERMON

Key #1
GOD'S KIND OF FAITH

He who is for you is a million times more than all that can be against you....What an advantage it would be if we could just come to a place where we know that everything is within reach of us.

Wigglesworth's faith was built on the fact that he "knew that he knew that he knew" that God was a million times greater than any difficulty or trial he came across. He lived in this reality of faith, which was such a great joy to him. This faith and the pursuit of this faith caused him to count all trials as joy. All of life became sweet to him with this outlook.

If you can even get just a glimpse of the beauty of this realm of faith, your whole life will change. If you see it, you will see the Christ-life, and you will give all so that you may have it. To live in this realm of faith is God's will and great desire for all of us.

This is the *"like precious faith"* (2 Peter 1:1) *"which was once for all delivered to the saints"* (Jude 3). This "faith that prevails," "the ever increasing faith," cannot be generated by anything else but seeing God through every situation and circumstance. It is the *"pearl of great price"* that the merchant found (Matthew 13:46).

No real joy is found in the faith built by man's precepts and programs. But there is exhilaration, *"joy inexpressible and full of glory"* (1 Peter 1:8), in the faith that God builds. The Lord Jesus is *"the author and finisher of our faith"* (Hebrews 12:2), and He will develop in us a joyful faith as we allow Him to do so.

God will develop in us a joyful faith as we allow Him to.

"He who has an ear, let him hear what the Spirit says to the churches" (Revelation 2:29). We must not settle for anything less than this reality of faith that is available to all of us—not just a mental assent or hope, but the faith that only asks once, believes, and sees its object come to pass.

You will not get it from any book. You will not get it from any seminar. You will not get it from any course or college or teacher. You will not get it from a television program, no matter how good it is. Although these things can instruct you, guide you, and help your faith to grow, you ultimately can get this kind of faith only from God Himself. From walking in close relationship with Him, living in His Word, hungering and thirsting for Him, and continuously yielding to His Spirit, you will obtain God's kind of faith as you learn to *"count it all joy"* (James 1:2).

Key #2:
"COUNT IT ALL JOY"

> God brings us into a place where the difficulties are, where the pressure is, where the hard corner is, where everything is so difficult that you know there are no possibilities on the human side—God must do it.

Have you ever been in the place where there are no possibilities that are humanly achievable? It is a hard place to be, for we are helpless. But it is also a blessed place because God must do it. Wigglesworth knew this place well, for it was in this place that he grew in real faith. He wanted his listeners to know its necessity and to understand it.

> *My brethren, count it all joy when you fall into various trials, knowing that the testing of your faith produces patience* [endurance].
> *(James 1:2–3)*

God wants to produce in us endurance and enduring faith, not "flash in the pan" faith. He wants marathon runners, not sprint racers, and we must know that enduring faith is produced through the fire of trial.

"Now faith is the substance of things hoped for, the evidence of things not seen" (Hebrews 11:1). It exists before the seen fact! *"Hope that is seen is not hope; for why does one still hope for what he sees?"* (Romans 8:24). Faith is an internal seeing, an internal knowing, a wonderful assurance that God is moving on our behalf. Faith is not psychological or emotional, nor is it positive thinking or feeling. It is that spiritual power, that spiritual force in you that causes things to change.

The key to finding joy in trials is knowing that God is giving us opportunities to exercise and increase our faith, to produce enduring faith. This increase of our faith must become our great delight and joy.

The fact is, *"the genuineness of your faith* [is] *much more precious than gold that perishes, though it is tested by fire"* (1 Peter 1:7)! More precious than gold? Gold is the most precious substance on earth to some. Another version renders James 1:2 as, *"Brothers,...welcome* [trials and temptations] *as friends"* (PHILLIPS). Is this possible? Are we actually to treat our trials, our hardships, our tests, our difficulties, as friends? As precious? Yes! A hundred times, yes!

Only in the *"refiner's fire"* (Malachi 3:2), in the fire of trial, are we changed. Every Christian must lay hold of this fact. As Wigglesworth stated in the above excerpt from his sermon, trials and difficulties bring us to the end of human answers so that we have to rely on God.

The nature of man is to walk by sight because it is natural and easy—it's the way we've always done things. However, the Bible tells us that God's way is to *"walk by faith, not by sight"* (2 Corinthians 5:7). If we are to do this, we need continual opportunities to exercise and use our faith.

When Paul wrote to Timothy to *"fight the good fight of faith"* (1 Timothy 6:12), he showed us that walking by faith and growing in faith is a *"good fight"*! And a fight is never won by ignoring the situation and doing nothing. No, a fight must be fought.

You are going through a fight right now. How do I know? Because everyone who wants to mature with God needs to grow in faith, and the only way to do this is to fight. Your battle may be against temptation and sin, against sickness, against the powers of hell trying to destroy your family, or in the financial area. Whatever it may be, it is a *"fight of faith,"* a ***"good fight of faith."*** Only by the faith of God will you conquer it.

> *Blessed is he that endures temptation* [trial, test, or attack], *for when he has been approved, he will receive the crown of life which the Lord has promised to those who love Him.*
> *(James 1:12)*

Welcome your fight, your trial, your test, as a challenge that will build your faith. Take the challenge. Rejoice that you have an opportunity to grow in faith, and thank God for the opportunity. Then seek Him earnestly in the Word and in prayer for the faith needed to win the fight. Each time you do this, each time you fight and win, you are further consumed by the Almighty.

Key #3
PERFECT LOVE

> Let me tell you what perfect love is: *"He who overcomes the world...believes that Jesus is the Son of God"* (1 John 5:5)....
>
> Perfect love means that Jesus has got a grip on your intentions, desires, and thoughts, and has purified everything. Perfect love cannot fear.

To be consumed by God is to be consumed by love. Wigglesworth's wonderful experience of life in the Spirit of God is expressed here: just as much as he was a man of great faith, so he was a man of great love.

Great heart love for Jesus is inseparably linked with true faith. This Wigglesworth knew and constantly communicated to others. Galatians 5:6 tells us that what really counts is the *"faith which worketh by love"* (KJV). We are looking for this real faith.

Now, two different kinds of faith are available to us: *"faith in God"* (Mark 11:22), and "natural faith," which is built in the realm of the soul. Yogis and others use this natural faith when they perform great feats. Cultists employ this soulish faith when they manifest some

> To be consumed by God is to be consumed by love.

counterfeit miracles and healings. The modern world calls it "positive thinking," with which so many millions in this generation—and even in the church—have become enamored.

But this natural faith is faith without God's love, and it pales into insignificance in the light of the *"faith in God"* of Mark 11:22. Paul wrote in 1 Corinthians 13:2, *"And though I have all faith, so that I could remove mountains, but have not love, I am nothing."* Soulish faith can even remove mountains! Remarkable! But even if we have natural faith to this degree, without love, we still are nothing.

The tragedy is that there are people, even some evangelists and ministers in the church today, operating in this faith; they are seeing some miraculous healings in their ministries, but they have lost their first love for God and their compassion for His people. The results keep them going, but deep down is a void, a lack of the real joy and fulfillment that they had when they began.

Tragically, at the end, some of us may be left saying, *"Lord, Lord, have we not prophesied in Your name...and done many wonders in Your name?"* only to hear the Lord reply, *"I never knew you; depart from Me"* (Matthew 7:22, 23). This is the tragic end of faith without love. The only answer is love, for when we come into perfect love, then fear that this might be the case cannot have any part of us. Love is how we know God and how He knows us.

The alternative to natural faith is faith in God, real faith. Not the faith of man, God's kind of faith is built on the Word of God by the Spirit of God. It is the *"faith which worketh by love"* (Galatians 5:6 KJV).

Wigglesworth operated in this godly faith—the faith that he indicated comes through possession. As he said, "Perfect love means that Jesus has got a grip on your intentions, desires, and thoughts, and has purified everything." Perfect love is being possessed by love, possessed by the Spirit of God. When this love begins to consume our hearts, we start to overcome the world!

This message is truly a word for the "last days." Jesus said in Matthew 24:12 that, in the last days, *"because lawlessness will abound, the love of many will grow cold."* We are seeing this in a very real way unfolding before us.

Build your relationship with God, study the Scriptures on love, pray that God increases love within you until you are totally consumed by perfect love. Your goal, your objective, must be to become a man or woman of great love, for this is the very nature of Christ within you. The major foundation of God in your life is that you be molded into His image.

Key #4
THE MOLDING OF GOD

Only melted gold is minted; only moistened clay is molded; only softened wax receives the seal; only broken and contrite hearts receive the mark as the Potter turns us on His wheel.

To be molded by the hand of God must become our everything, our all-consuming desire. When it is, every trial is a blessing, because in everything we see the opportunity to trust Him to purify us further. As we are able to discern the truth and live as melted gold, as moistened clay, as softened wax, with broken and contrite hearts, we are pliable in the Potter's hands, as He conforms us to His image.

Unfortunately, too many do not realize these principles. They have heard a message of "come to Jesus and everything will work out; everything will be all right." Many are not told that God loves them too much to leave them as they are, that the great privilege He has for them is that they are to be changed into *"the image of His Son"* (Romans 8:29).

To be transformed so that Christ is revealed to others through us is a blessing beyond anything known to man! However, too often it is lost in the superficial preaching meant to please *"itching ears"* (2 Timothy 4:3).

Christ is returning for His bride, *"a glorious church, not having spot or wrinkle or any such thing, but that she should be holy and without blemish"* (Ephesians 5:27). So we know that there must be tremendous preparation of His bride, the church, before His return. The message and reality of the *"refiner's fire"* (Malachi 3:2), the "potter's wheel," the preciousness of trial, is such a major part of that preparation. God used Wigglesworth

The time of Christ's coming is at hand, and we must be ready.

to declare this message, which will be declared increasingly in these last days, because the time is at hand and the bride must be ready.

My friend, rejoice! Rejoice in the hands of the Potter until you are completely molded and possessed by His Spirit.

Key #5
THE MARK OF THE HIGH CALLING

Brother, sister, if God brings you into oneness and the fellowship with the most high God, your nature will quiver in His presence....There is a sanctification of the Spirit where the thoughts are holy, where the life is beautiful with no blemish.

How beautiful a thing our brother talked about in this passage! So much of Wigglesworth's preaching comes back to the wonder of being possessed by the Holy Spirit, which was the secret of His life and walk of power. It is also the key for our lives if we are to walk in power. In nearly every message, he tries to impart this idea to God's people, for it is the mark that we must aim for. This *"prize of the upward call of God in Christ Jesus"* (Philippians 3:14)—being possessed by the Holy Spirit—means His absolute Lordship, our complete surrender, oneness with God, sanctification, rest, and power. It is the ultimate end of our purification by the *"refiner's fire"* (Malachi 3:2), the profound purpose of the molding of the hand of God.

Paul wrote to the Philippians, *"Forgetting those things which are behind and reaching forward to those things which are ahead, I press toward the goal for the prize of the upward call of God in Christ Jesus"* (3:13–14).

Reaching forth! Pressing toward! This is what it means to be *"a flame of fire"* (Hebrews 1:7), burning to be one with the Most High. Our very nature quivers in His presence here where life is beautiful!

God is calling His church to walk in this reality in the last days. Wigglesworth, like Paul, saw it and tasted of it. He lived it, and out of the living came the message.

You can live it, too. You can! Will you make it your goal and be part of the "end-times army" that God is raising up right now for the great final harvest?

Key #6
THE HUNGER FOR TRANSFORMATION

Perhaps you have been counting it all sadness until now. Never mind; you turn the scale, and you will get a lot more out of it, more than you ever had before.

Whether you have just come to Jesus or have walked with Him for many years, this revelation to *"count it all joy"* (James 1:2) must become yours. "Perhaps you have been counting it all sadness until now," but you are now beginning to grasp this revelation, beginning to see the purposes of God, and you desire to start living in His realm. Doing so is not easy, even for the seriously hungry.

A desperate hunger for transformation must come within you. Today's world is directly opposed to this transformation. The spirit of this age is so powerfully against God's people being possessed by the Holy Spirit that only the desperate—the ones who cry out in earnestness to God, the ones who are made ill by compromise and complacency—will break through to this place God so much desires for His people.

Transformation does not take grand gifts; it takes great guts.

It does not take intelligence; it takes integrity. It does not take grand gifts; it takes great guts. It takes hunger and holiness, desperate desire and discipline.

Jesus asked, *"When the Son of Man comes, will He really find faith on the earth?"* (Luke 18:8). He knew the spirit of this last-days age and the spiritual opposition that we would be facing. When we see many churches, in spite of their efforts, *"grow cold"* (Matthew 24:12), there must come a cry from our inward parts for transformation. We need to adopt the heart-cry of David when he said,

> *Hear my cry, O God; attend to my prayer.*
> *From the end of the earth I will cry to You,*
> *when my heart is overwhelmed; lead me to the*
> *rock that is higher than I.   (Psalm 61:1–2)*

Like David, Wigglesworth did not just pray; he did not just ask. Rather, he cried out to God with weeping and tears—tears that flowed from a dissatisfied heart, a heart that cried, *"I shall be satisfied when I awake in Your likeness"* (Psalm 17:15).

> I believe that a real weeping would be good for us. You are in a poor way if you cannot weep. I do thank God for my tears.

Chapter Six

FILLED WITH GOD

PROLOGUE

❧

Every Soul

The two policemen grabbed Wigglesworth and started pushing him through the crowd. He had arrived in Norway only that morning, but word of him had spread before his arrival. Thousands surrounded the town hall hoping to get inside, but unfortunately not another person could fit. Packed in like sardines, the people inside were so tightly squeezed together that no one could have tripped and fallen to the ground.

Having heard the rumors that a man who was able to perform miracles would be there, people had flocked to the hall from far and wide. Many were not Christians, but they had come to witness and to seek the healings and other miraculous events that might happen.

With much difficulty, the policemen struggled to get Wigglesworth to the front of the hall. As he stood on the platform looking out over the vast crowd, he was consumed with such tremendous zeal for the Lord and compassion for the people that he cried out, "God, give me a message that's different, that something might happen here that is different from anything else."

As Wigglesworth began to preach, the voice of God inwardly spoke to him, "If you will ask Me, I will give you every soul." Had he heard God correctly? He continued to preach. "If you will ask Me, I will give you every soul." He struggled. He knew now it was the voice of the Lord, but he was slow to respond.

Once again the message came, "If you believe and ask Me, I will give you every soul."

Wigglesworth stopped. Every eye was upon him. Why had he stopped preaching? With his eyes closed, he prayed, "All right, Lord, please do it. I ask You, please give me every soul."

From every direction a wind seemed to blow—the breath of the Holy Spirit swept over the auditorium from the front to the back. People all over the town hall began crying out to God for mercy. Every man, woman, and child became acutely aware of personal sinfulness and unworthiness before this awesome God whom they were now experiencing. As they begged God's forgiveness, Wigglesworth pointed them to Jesus and the way of salvation.

With all of them yielding to Christ, God saved every soul just as He had spoken to this man who was "filled with God."[1]

FILLED WITH GOD

****

Filled with God
A Message by Smith Wigglesworth

To begin, I want to read to you the second chapter of Hebrews.

> *Therefore we must give the more earnest heed to the things we have heard, lest we drift away. For if the word spoken through angels proved steadfast, and every transgression and disobedience received a just reward, how shall we escape if we neglect so great a salvation, which at the first began to be spoken by the Lord, and was confirmed to us by those who heard Him, God also bearing witness both with signs and wonders, with various miracles, and gifts of the Holy Spirit, according to His own will? For He has not put the world to come, of which we speak, in subjection to angels. But one testified in a certain place, saying: "What is man that You are mindful of him, or the son of man that You take care of him? You have made him a little lower than the angels; You have crowned him with glory and honor, and set him over the works of Your hands. You have put*

all things in subjection under his feet." For in that He put all in subjection under him, He left nothing that is not put under him. But now we do not yet see all things put under him. But we see Jesus, who was made a little lower than the angels, for the suffering of death crowned with glory and honor, that He, by the grace of God, might taste death for everyone. For it was fitting for Him, for whom are all things and by whom are all things, in bringing many sons to glory, to make the captain of their salvation perfect through sufferings. For both He who sanctifies and those who are being sanctified are all of one, for which reason He is not ashamed to call them brethren, saying: "I will declare Your name to My brethren; in the midst of the assembly I will sing praise to You." And again: "I will put My trust in Him." And again: "Here am I and the children whom God has given Me." Inasmuch then as the children have partaken of flesh and blood, He Himself likewise shared in the same, that through death He might destroy him who had the power of death, that is, the devil, and release those who through fear of death were all their lifetime subject to bondage. For indeed He does not give aid to angels, but He does give aid to the seed of Abraham. Therefore, in all things He had to be made like His brethren, that He might be a merciful and faithful High Priest in things pertaining to God, to make propitiation for the sins of the people. For in that He Himself has suffered, being tempted, He is able to aid those who are tempted.
(Hebrews 2:1–18)

Now this, like every other Scripture, is all very important for us. You could scarcely, at the beginning, pick any special verse out of this we have read. It is all so full of truth; it means so much to us. We must understand that God in these times wants to bring us into perfect life, that we need never, under any circumstances, go outside of His Word for anything.

Some people come with only a very small thought concerning God's fullness, and a lot of people are satisfied with a thimbleful. You can just imagine God saying, "Oh, if they only knew how much they could take away!"

Other people come with a larger vessel, and they go away satisfied. But you can feel how much God is longing for us to have such a desire for more—such a longing as only God Himself can satisfy.

I suppose you women would have a good idea of what I mean from the illustration of a screaming child being handed about from one to another, but never satisfied until it gets to the bosom of its mother. You will find that there is no peace, no help, no source of strength, no power, no life, nothing that can satisfy the cry of the child of God but the Word of God.

God has a special way of satisfying the cry of His children. He is waiting to open to us the windows of heaven until He has so moved in the depths of our hearts that everything that is unlike Himself has been destroyed.

No one in this place today needs to go away dry, dry. God wants you to be filled. My brother, my sister, God wants you today to be like a watered garden, filled with the fragrance of His own heavenly joy, until, at least, you know you have touched immensity.

The Son of God came for no other purpose than to lift and lift, and mold and fashion and remold, until we are shaped in the image of His mind.

I know that the dry ground can have floods, and may God save me from ever wanting anything less than a flood. I will not stoop for small things when I have such a big God. Through the blood of Christ's atonement, we may have untold riches. We need the warming atmosphere of the Spirit's power to bring us closer and closer until nothing but God can satisfy. Then we may have some idea of what God has left after we have taken our fill.

It is only like a sparrow taking a drink of the ocean and then looking around and saying, "What a vast ocean! What a lot more I could have taken if I had only had room." You may sometimes have things you can use and not know it.

Don't you know that you could be dying of thirst right in a river of plenty?

There was once a vessel in the mouth of the Amazon river. They thought they were still in the ocean, and they were dying of thirst; some of them were nearly mad. They saw a ship and asked if they would give them some water, for some of them were dying of thirst, and they heard the reply, "Dip your bucket right over. You are in the mouth of the river."

There are any number of people today in the midst of a great river of life, but they are dying of thirst because they do not dip down and take it. Beloved, you may have the Word, but you need an awakened spirit.

The Word is not alive until it is moved upon by the Spirit of God, and in the right sense it becomes Spirit and life when it is touched by His hand alone.

Oh, beloved, there is a stream that *"shall make glad the city of God"* (Psalm 46:4). There is a stream of life that makes everything move.

There is a touch of divine life and likeness through the Word of God that comes from nowhere else. There is a death that has no life in it, and there is a death-likeness with Christ that is full of life.

O beloved, there is no such thing as an end to God's beginnings. But we must be in it; we must know it. It is the Holy One dwelling in the temple *"not made with hands"* (2 Corinthians 5:1). O beloved, He touches, and it is done. He is the same God over all, *"rich to all who call upon Him"* (Romans 10:12).

Pentecost is the last thing that God has to touch the earth with. The baptism is that last thing; if you do not get this, you are living in a weak and impoverished condition that is no good to yourself or anybody else.

May God move us on to a place where there is no measure to this fullness that He wants to give us. God exalted Jesus and gave Him a name above every name (Philippians 2:9). You notice that everything has been put under Him (Ephesians 1:22).

It has been about eight years since I was last in Oakland. In that time, I have seen thousands healed by the power of God. In Sweden, during the last five months of last year, we saw over 7,000 people saved by the power of God. The tide is rolling in. Let us see to it today that we get right out into the tide, for it will bear us.

The bosom of God's love is the center of all things. Get your eyes off yourself; lift them up high and see the Lord, for in the Lord there is everlasting strength (Isaiah 26:4).

If you went to see a doctor, the more you told him, the more he would know. But when you come to Doctor Jesus, He knows all from the beginning, and He never gives you the wrong medicine.

I went to visit a sick one today, and someone said, "Here is a person who has been poisoned through and through by a doctor giving him the wrong medicine." Jesus sends His healing power and brings His restoring grace, and so there is nothing to fear.

The only thing that is wrong is your wrong conception of the mightiness of His redemption. He was wounded so that He might be touched with a feeling of your infirmities (Hebrews 4:15 KJV). He took your flesh and laid it upon the cross, so that *"He might destroy him who had the power of death, that is, the devil, and release those who through fear of death were all their lifetime subject to bondage"* (Hebrews 2:14–15).

You will find that almost all of the ailments that you are heir to come through satanic lines, and they must be cast out. Do not listen to what Satan says to you, for the Devil is a liar from the beginning (John 8:44). If people would only listen to the truth of God, they would find out they have power over the Devil, over all satanic forces; they would realize that every evil spirit is subject to them; they would find out that they are always in the place of triumph; and they would *"reign in life"* (Romans 5:17) by King Jesus.

Never live in a lesser place than where God has called you to, and He has called you up on high to live with Him. God has designed that everything shall be subject to man. Through Christ, He has given you power *"over all the power of the enemy"* (Luke 10:19). He has worked out your eternal redemption.

I was finishing a meeting one day in Switzerland. When we had concluded the meeting and had ministered to all the sick, we went out to see some people. Two boys came to inform us that there was a blind man present at the meeting that afternoon who had heard all the words of the preacher and said he was surprised that he had not been prayed for. They went on to say that this blind man had heard so much that he would not leave that place until he could see.

I said, "This is positively unique. God will do something today for that man."

We got to the place. This blind man said he never had seen. He had been born blind, but because of the Word preached in the afternoon, he was not going home until he could see.

If I ever have joy, it is when I have a lot of people who will not be satisfied until they get all they have come for. With great joy, I anointed him that day and laid hands on his eyes, and then immediately God opened his eyes.

It was very strange how he acted. There were some electric lights; first he counted them. Then he counted us. Oh, the ecstatic pleasure that every moment was created in that man because of his sight! It made us all feel like weeping and dancing and shouting.

Then he pulled out his watch and said that for years he had been feeling the watch for the time by the raised figures, but now he could look at it and tell us the time. Then, looking as if he was awakened from some deep sleep or some long, strange dream, he awakened to the fact that he had never seen the faces of his father and mother, and he went to the door and rushed out.

At night, he was the first in the meeting. All the people knew him as the blind man, and I had to give him a long time to talk about his new sight.

Beloved, I wonder how much you want to take away today. You could not carry it if it were substance, but there is something about the grace and power and blessings of God that can be carried, no matter how big they are.

Oh, what a Savior! What a place we are in, by grace, that He may come in to commune with us. He is willing to say to every heart, *"Peace, be still!"* (Mark 4:39), and to every weak body, *"Be strong"* (1 Corinthians 16:13).

Are you going halfway, or are you going right to the end? Be not deceived today by Satan, but believe God.

****

LIFE KEYS FROM THE SERMON

Key #1
GOD'S LONGING FOR YOU

Some people come with only a very small thought concerning God's fullness, and a lot of people are satisfied with a thimbleful. You can just imagine God saying, "Oh, if they only knew how much they could take away!"

Other people come with a larger vessel, and they go away satisfied. But you can feel how much God is longing for us to have such a desire for more—such a longing as only God Himself can satisfy.

"Smith Wigglesworth was a man filled with love, filled with compassion, filled with faith, filled with God."[2] How easily we lower the standard he set for us, yet how much God wants to raise it again. He wants to let us know we can have as much as we are able to take away.

This message, in these last days, must ring out again loud and clear for all to hear. Now more than ever, God's prophets are needed to stand and stir up dissatisfaction in the hearts of believers around the world and to generate fervent hunger for more of God, for more of His anointing, for more of His power, for more of His blessing in every way.

> Too many Christians today are satisfied with only a "thimbleful" of the Spirit.

Too many "thimbleful" Christians exist today, who are satisfied with just a thimble's worth of the Spirit. They come with a hunger only the size of a thimble, and they receive accordingly. Some have a cup-sized hunger and some the capacity of a bowl, but God is longing to raise up an army of "bucketful," "barrelful," and "tankful" Christians—men and women who will move in the anointing and power of the Lord as Wigglesworth did.

This is God's longing for you, to take as much as you can from what He has provided for you, to ever hunger for more. God is after the heart, the affections, the depth of a man. His longing for you is that you long for Him, and that you long to be filled with His fullness. Be filled with God!

Key #2
SAVE ME FROM SETTLING FOR LESS!

I know that the dry ground can have floods, and may God save me from ever wanting anything less than a flood.

"Save me, God, from ever wanting anything less than a flood." Oh, that this might become the cry of our hearts!

Wigglesworth was never satisfied with just a thimbleful, a cupful, a bucketful, or even a tankful of the Holy Spirit. He yearned for a constant flood. If his desire ever lessened, he knew he was backsliding.

When preaching in New York, he often visited Niagara Falls. Friends who went with him tell of him standing before the Falls, with tears running down his cheeks, crying, "Like that, Lord, like that, in me."[3]

"Whet our appetites, Lord. Save us from ever decreasing in desire for You." This must become our prayer if we want to stay in God's plan for our lives. The victorious Christian life must have a continuously increasing desire with no lessening.

Many think that to be backslidden is to have totally gone back into sin, but backsliding is a thing of the heart—not always noticeable on the surface—marked by an apathy of spirit and loss of hunger for God. It is very possible to backslide facing forward. Christians who have had a cupful in the past, yet now are satisfied with a thimbleful, are backslidden, as well as those who were at the bucketful stage but have regressed to expecting only a cupful.

Too many Christians today are living on the echo of yesterday, on the echo of something that once was—a relationship they once had with God, an anointing they once moved in. Yet they are powerless because the echo is just a shallow reflection of the real thing, a mere memory that has no power for the present.

Are you living on an echo of something that once was? If so, you need to turn around *"and do the first works"* (Revelation 2:5). Don't be satisfied with anything less than the level of desire and anointing that you once knew. Then the Lord will restore your joy, *"that your joy may be full"* (John 16:24).

Friend, God has *"joy inexpressible and full of glory"* (1 Peter 1:8) that can take you beyond any despair and lift you up above any circumstance. But you must get back to God's plan for your life and leave your own plan alone. God's plan and purpose for you is that you have an ever increasing love and desire for Him.

Save us, God, from ever wanting anything less than everything that you have for us. Let there be a continual flood of your Spirit pouring through us, so that we may be as this man was, *"filled with all the fullness of God"* (Ephesians 3:19).

Key #3
AN AWAKENED SPIRIT

You may have the Word, but you need an awakened spirit.
    The Word is not alive until it is moved upon by the Spirit of God.

Like the sailors in the mouth of the Amazon, many Christians are dying of spiritual lack in the midst of the abundant riches of God. In this present time, more of the preaching of the Word of God provides more revelation of the Word than in any previous era. The wonderful truths and promises of God are being declared in churches around the world by men of God with sincere hearts.

However, great teaching becomes just *"knowledge* [that] *puffs up"* (1 Corinthians 8:1) in the minds of those whose spirits have fallen into slumber. An awakened spirit is one that is free of the doping effects of the flesh and the carnal mind.

Who you are and what is yours now in Christ is nothing short of phenomenal! But the carnal mind (the sinful, fleshly mind that you lived with prior to conversion) cannot even begin to see this, let alone appreciate it. Neither can you grasp it if you are still controlled by your emotions and feelings. The reason is that, when your emotions rule, your spirit slumbers. When you feel happy, you think you believe; but when you are sad, down, or depressed, the faith you thought you had seems to disappear. You are riding an emotional roller coaster—up, then down; belief, then doubt; trust, then worry, and so on.

> Who and what you are in Christ is nothing short of phenomenal!

The solution is to live by your born-again spirit, an awakened spirit ruled by the Holy Spirit, and not by your mind and emotions. But how do you do this?

As spiritual hunger grows, causing us to earnestly seek God in the Word and in prayer, our spirits break the shackles of the flesh and of the soul (the mind and emotions). We begin to live with an awakened spirit that lays hold of all the *"exceedingly great and precious promises"* (2 Peter 1:4) of God. This, in turn, brings us into the realization of the power and authority that we actually have in Him. We begin to live on high!

All the truths and keys in this book are to this end. Wigglesworth lived with this awakened spirit.

God is looking for those who will do the same. Lord, let us ever live with an awakened spirit. Take us out of our slumber, so that we might be all that You desire—totally filled with all that You have for us.

Key #4
LIVING ON HIGH

> Never live in a lesser place than where God has called you to, and He has called you up on high to live with Him....Through Christ, He has given you power *"over all the power of the enemy"* (Luke 10:19).

God wants His people to live in the place of authority! Absolute dominion in the spirit realm. He has called us to *"reign with Him"* (2 Timothy 2:12), to reign with the King of Kings and the Lord of Lords!

He said, *"All authority ["power," KJV] has been given to Me in heaven and on earth"* (Matthew 28:18). This is the power that is ours as we become one with Him. Certainly, the Enemy has power. But we have *"all power"*! All power over the Enemy and our own flesh. Wigglesworth lived in it, and so can we.

God wants us to live in the place where we wield this power. We have power over the power of the Enemy, but all too many believers live under the power of the Enemy—under sickness, under poverty, under bondage to sin. *"Brethren, these things ought not to be so"* (James 3:10). What Wigglesworth was saying was, never settle for anything less than complete victory.

It is one thing to be going through a trial fighting, but quite another to be stuck having resigned oneself to it. Too many have grown to accept their difficulties. Why? The *"spirit of slumber"* (Romans 11:8 KJV) that they have allowed to overtake them does not permit them to see or hear anything differently.

Do you again see Wigglesworth's secret in the above excerpt from his sermon? He didn't accept anything less than God's best. The secret of the *"flame of fire"* (Hebrews 1:7) is the secret of being filled with God!

> The hunger
> brings the desperation,
> brings the breakthrough,
> brings the awakened spirit,
> brings the revelation,
> brings the authority,
> brings the power,
> brings the victory,
> brings everything God has for us
> and everything that we'll ever need,
> until we are totally filled with God.

You can live *"on high"* (Hebrews 1:3) with Him and *"reign with Him"* (2 Timothy 2:12) as you are filled with God.

Key #5
DON'T LEAVE

If I ever have joy, it is when I have a lot of people who will not be satisfied until they get all they have come for.

Never be satisfied until you possess what you came for! If we confined Wigglesworth's teaching to a few major points, this would surely be one of them.

The tenacity of faith, the refusing to be satisfied with anything less than God's best, the standing and believing—this is the faith that pleases God. It was the faith of the little woman with the issue of blood who said, *"If only I may touch His clothes, I shall be made well"* (Mark 5:28). Even though there was a great multitude to press through, and even though she was surely shunned repeatedly in her pursuit because she was considered unclean, you can still hear her saying, "If I can only....I will not stop until I touch Him....I won't leave until I am whole." True to the faith in her heart and the words of her mouth, she was healed! This again is an aspect of that special faith—the faith of God that God wants in you.

> The tenacity of faith that refuses to be satisfied with anything less than God's best is the faith that pleases Him.

Jacob illustrated this kind of tenacity in the natural when, wrestling with *"a Man"* all night, he cried out, *"I will not let You go unless You bless me!"* (Genesis 32:24, 26). The terrible pain from his hip being dislocated and the exhaustion he must have experienced from the long fight did not deter him. Jacob was focused on one thing only—being blessed by the Almighty—and he was not letting go until he received the blessing.

God had built that desire in Jacob for the blessing; He gave him the supernatural strength to fight for it; and in the end, God left Jacob permanently marked with a limp as a physical reminder that He had touched him spiritually. May we all allow God to create that same kind of hunger in us, a desire so strong that we won't quit until we are fully saturated with our Lord.

Why did it bring Wigglesworth so much joy when he found someone who said, "I won't leave until I get it.....*I will not let You go unless You bless me!'*"? Because this is what he preached and lived for: to build this kind of faith in as many people as he could—this radical, unrelenting, uncompromising, no-retreating faith. When he saw it rise up within someone, he saw the fulfillment of his purpose and the end of his labors.

This heart attitude combines the burning desire for God to move, the utter dissatisfaction with the present condition, and steadfast *"faith in God"* (Mark 11:22). This kind of faith was written about previously in this book, and even more so on the pages of Wigglesworth's life.

Truly instilling and nurturing faith in others was the fruit of his life and ministry, and therefore brought him the joy that only God can give. We know that faith is what pleases our heavenly Father, for *"without faith it is impossible to please Him"* (Hebrews 11:6). Wigglesworth had become so consumed with God that what was God's greatest joy became his greatest joy. I pray that in your pursuit of God's best, it may become your greatest joy, also.

What have you come for? Will you leave this book without it? Will the standard on these pages—the power, keys, and principles—become yours? Will you say, "I will not leave until I have them! I won't leave until I am absolutely and totally filled with God"? What have you come for, and what will you take away?

Final Key
CHOOSE YOUR LIFE STANDARD

Beloved, I wonder how much you want to take away today....

Are you going halfway, or are you going right to the end?

Beloved, this book is dedicated to you. As the book began by talking about hunger for God, so it ends by asking how much you want. How much you get from this book is entirely up to you and how hungry you are. Read it through until you have what it has to give. I wonder how much you will take from it.

There is a standard on these pages that God wants to lift you to. I believe it is the spiritual standard for God's glorious church, His "end-times army" that will reap the great end-times harvest. It is the standard of the *"flame of fire"* (Hebrews 1:7), the standard of being "consumed and possessed" by the Spirit.

I first saw the standard years ago when the Holy Spirit told me to read the pages of Smith Wigglesworth's life. I hungered for it, I thirsted for it, and I set myself to see it realized in my own life. Having the vision of this standard before me radically changed my life and drove me deeper into God. It still does.

There are times when I have despaired of it, being surrounded by "witnesses" of a far lesser standard and allowing myself to accept that lesser standard. But I have decided, according to Hebrews 12:1,

> We all need the standard of these great "eagles" of God, because there are a lot of "chickens" out there.

to surround myself with a *"great...cloud of witnesses,"* to surround myself with the champions of Hebrews 11—the great men and women of the "faith hall of fame"—and the modern day champions of faith, of whom there are many.

I have decided that their standard will become mine. I accept nothing less, for I know that the standard I look to is the standard I will rise to or be limited by.

It has been said, "If you want to fly with the eagles, don't run with the chickens." If you want to fly with the eagles, you must surround yourself with eagles and learn from them. We all need the standard of these great "eagles" of God, because there are a lot of "chickens" out there.

"Since we are surrounded by so great a cloud of witnesses" (Hebrews 12:1). Wigglesworth was a great witness. His life was, and still is, a tremendous challenge to us. Now he leaves us with a challenge. "Beloved, I wonder how much you want to take away today."

We have learned so many wonderful truths and lessons from Wigglesworth's messages, life, and ministry. Keys on hunger, obedience, yieldedness, possession, rejoicing in trials, brokenness, and real faith. What will we do with them?

To be *"a flame of fire"* (Hebrews 1:7), ever burning, is within the reach of every believer who will heed the call and take up the challenge. "Are you going halfway, or are you going right to the end?" For some, the challenge of this book, the spiritual standard set by it and the keys it gives, will change their lives forever. For others, it will sadly remain just another interesting book to have on the shelf.

Gideon had many more soldiers than those who finally went to war and took part in that glorious victory. I believe that Gideon's army is a picture of God's "end-times army." In the same way, though many are at hand, only those who take up the challenge, who are totally sold out to the battle, will reap the great end-times harvest.

Beloved, again, this book is dedicated to you. It is not a *"milk"* book, but a *"solid food* ["*meat,*" KJV]" book (1 Corinthians 3:2). It is not for baby Christians, or for the lukewarm; rather, it is for the serious believers who long to reach their maximum potential in Christ.

A great battle lies ahead against the forces of darkness that are even now gathering with great intensity against God's people, with the rise of false prophets, the New Age movement, and ultimately "the beast." But there is also a great victory to be won.

You have heard the call. You have felt the challenge. You have sensed the thrill of the potential that is within you. Now it is up to you. You can be filled with God just as Wigglesworth was. You can be *"a flame of fire"* in God's "end-times army."

Smith Wigglesworth went to be with the Lord on the twelfth of March, 1947. He never stopped yearning and burning for his Master, and he served and ministered right up until that day. His passing was like taking a simple step from this reality to the next. He was in full health one minute, talking with an old friend. Then, in the next instant, he left this earthly existence to be in the presence of Almighty God to spend eternity in ultimate joy and receive the crown laid up for him.

Now the question remains, Who will take up the torch Wigglesworth laid aside? Will you respond to the inward call of the Holy Spirit to become *"a flame of fire,"* ablaze with this same passion for the Lord?

Notes

Editor's Note: The biographical information and miraculous events of Wigglesworth's ministry have been recorded by several authors. In cases where information has not been directly quoted, the following citations are the most complete or primary sources found for the particular topic.

Chapter 1

[1] Albert Hibbert, *Smith Wigglesworth: The Secret of His Power* (Tulsa, OK: Harrison House, 1993), 42–44.
[2] William Hacking, *Smith Wigglesworth Remembered* (Tulsa, OK: Harrison House, 1981), 35.
[3] Hibbert, 59.
[4] George Stormont, *Smith Wigglesworth: A Man Who Walked with God* (Tulsa, OK: Harrison House, 1989), 49.

Chapter 2

[1] Smith Wigglesworth, *Ever Increasing Faith* (Springfield, MO: Gospel Publishing House, 1971), 65–66.
[2] Stanley H. Frodsham, *Smith Wigglesworth: Apostle of Faith* (Springfield, MO: Gospel Publishing House, 1990), 23, 83.
[3] Stormont, 31.
[4] Frodsham, 112.

Chapter 3

[1] Frodsham, 80.
[2] Smith Wigglesworth, *Faith That Prevails* (Springfield, MO: Gospel Publishing House, 1966), 32–34.
[3] Frodsham, 45.
[4] Hacking, 74.
[5] Colin Whittaker, *Seven Pentecostal Pioneers* (Springfield, MO: Gospel Publishing House, 1985), 24–25.

Notes, continued

Chapter 4

[1] Frodsham, 58–60.
[2] Frodsham, 111.
[3] Hacking, 19.
[4] Hibbert, 29–30.
[5] Wigglesworth, *Faith That Prevails*, 12–13
[6] Wigglesworth, *Faith That Prevails*, 11.

Chapter 5

[1] Jack Hywel-Davies, *The Life of Smith Wigglesworth* (Ann Arbor, MI: Servant Publications, 1987), 92.
[2] Frodsham, 135.
[3] Hacking, 35.
[4] Frodsham, 17.
[5] Stormont, 112.
[6] Stormont, 65.
[7] Wigglesworth, *Faith That Prevails*, 11.
[8] Hacking, 90.
[9] Frodsham, 137.
[10] Frodsham, 139.

Chapter 6

[1] Frodsham, 77–78.
[2] Hacking, 61.
[3] Frodsham, 146.

SUGGESTED READING

Frodsham, Stanley H. *Smith Wigglesworth: Apostle of Faith*. Springfield, MO: Gospel Publishing House, 1990.

Hacking, William. *Smith Wigglesworth Remembered*. Tulsa, OK: Harrison House, 1981.

Hibbert, Albert. *Smith Wigglesworth: The Secret of His Power*. Tulsa, OK: Harrison House, 1993.

Hywel-Davies, Jack. *The Life of Smith Wigglesworth*. Ann Arbor, MI: Servant Publications, 1988.

Stormont, George. *Smith Wigglesworth: A Man Who Walked with God*. Tulsa, OK: Harrison House, 1989.

Whittaker, Colin. *Seven Pentecostal Pioneers*. Springfield, MO: Gospel Publishing House, 1985.

Wigglesworth, Smith. *Faith That Prevails*. Springfield, MO: Gospel Publishing House, 1966.

ABOUT THE AUTHOR

During the past fifteen years, Peter J. Madden has served as pastor, evangelist, camp and conference speaker, and worship leader. After pioneering churches in both Australia and the United States, he now travels internationally, preaching the message of the Cross in crusades, conferences, and churches throughout Asia, Europe, America, and Africa.

Peter was born in 1961 in Sydney, Australia. His interest in evangelist Smith Wigglesworth was sparked when he first heard Wigglesworth's name, and the Holy Spirit instructed him that he was to go and learn about him. In 1989, after pastoring a church in Wollongong, Australia, he and his family traveled to California and were led by God to an old missionary home in Oakland where many great men and women of the faith had stayed in years past. It was there, in an old cupboard in the front room of the house, that he discovered thirty-seven of Smith Wigglesworth's messages. These sermons are the basis for both this book and his second book, *The Secret of Wigglesworth's Power* (also published by Whitaker House).

He has established Flames of Fire Ministries to help others kindle the same kind of fire and commitment to God that Wigglesworth and other great revivalists had, so that they also may glorify God and serve others powerfully in the love of Christ.

Peter J. Madden
Flames of Fire Ministries
P.O. Box 3663
Robina, T.C., Queensland, Australia 4230

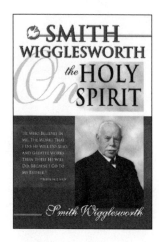

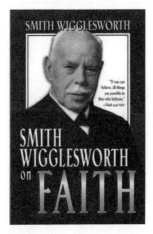

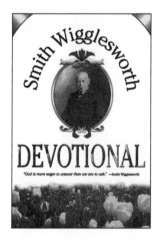

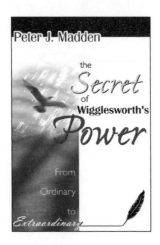